CW00481696

# My life in Food

# ALBERT ROUX

# My life in Food

## A Memoir

**WN**
WEIDENFELD & NICOLSON

First published in Great Britain in 2022 by Weidenfeld & Nicolson
an imprint of The Orion Publishing Group Ltd
Carmelite House, 50 Victoria Embankment
London EC4Y 0DZ
An Hachette UK Company

1 3 5 7 9 10 8 6 4 2

Copyright © Albert Roux 2022

The right of Albert Roux to be identified as the author
of this work have been asserted in accordance
with the Copyright, Designs and Patents Act of 1988

Grateful thanks to the Roux family for permission to
reproduce the photos on pp. 2, 6, 10, 17, 27, 32, 37, 47,
48, 54, 56, 58-9, 61, 62, 65, 67, 81, 84, 86 and 156.

All rights reserved. No part of this publication may be
reproduced, stored in a retrieval system, or transmitted
in any form or by any means, electronic, mechanical,
photocopying, recording, or otherwise, without the
prior permission of both the copyright owner and the
above publisher of this book.

A CIP catalogue record for this book is
available from the British Library.

ISBN (Hardback) 9781474617765
ISBN (eBook) 9781474617789
ISBN (Audio) 9781474617796

Typeset by Bryony Clark
Printed and bound in Great Britain
by Clays Ltd, Elcograf, S.p.A

www.weidenfeldandnicolson.co.uk

MIX
Paper from
responsible sources
FSC® C104740
www.fsc.org

www.orionbooks.co.uk

# CONTENTS

# LIST OF ILLUSTRATIONS

# EDITOR'S NOTE

Towards the end of 2019, at the age of 83, Albert Roux started working on his memoir. He had often been encouraged to publish an autobiography over the years, and finally felt that the right time had come. This was no retirement project: he was still a busy man, involved in running his Chez Roux group of restaurants, and with many different consultancies, charities and enterprises on the go. While he wanted to tell his story, he didn't want to undertake the book all alone, so I came in to help him put it together. They were wonderful meetings, Albert's natural charisma and courtesy cut through always by a mischievous streak, and the task was made easy by the fact that he was a natural storyteller, interested in everything, with a sharp memory and a vivid turn of phrase.

Progress was swift, until the pandemic came. It was catastrophic for his industry and naturally slowed down his progress on the book, not least because Zoom meetings were never going to be the right medium for such a convivial man. Nevertheless he did continue working on it, even through the sad loss of his brother Michel, and the various lockdowns which forced the temporary closure of his beloved restaurants. At our last meeting he was impatient with the restrictions that Covid had brought and worried for the future of his businesses, but undiminished and forceful as ever.

In January 2021, Albert died. As for the memoir, sadly he had not lived to finish it completely. But the story that was already on paper was an amazing one: it took him from his boyhood in wartime France, to the dazzling success of the early years at the Gavroche. In the process it shone a light on the process of a food culture that has changed out of all recognition, in large part because of his own astonishing talents. It would have been a travesty not to have published the book, but it felt incomplete without the last part of the story. His son, Michel Jr, kindly agreed to provide an afterword to bring his father's life right up to the end, and contributions from family and friends helped to flesh out some detail.

It is a great shame that Albert didn't live to see his book published. But it is a privilege to be able to bring you his story in his own voice; energetic, funny, determined and vigorous to the end.

Celia Hayley
London, 2022

# ACKNOWLEDGEMENTS

I am very grateful to many people for ensuring that my father's book could be published as he wanted. Many thanks to his agent Andrew Nurnberg who encouraged him to tell his story; to Alan Samson and Ed Lake at Weidenfeld & Nicolson for receiving the book with such enthusiasm; to Celia Hayley, for helping him put it together; to Edwina Simon and Katie Crowther for their assistance; to Marc Beaujeu, Steven Doherty, Silvano Giraldin and my mother Monique Roux who all offered their time and memories; to Anne Marie Ruthven Murray for everything she did for my father; to Abdul for his kindness and patience driving him to his lunches and occasionally helping to put his socks on; and to Maria and Josh for making Dad happy beyond words with their love and affection for him.

*Michel Roux Jr*

# Childhood

# 1

## Childhood

Of course, everything I know of my very early childhood I know from my mother. At the time of my birth, she worked in the charcuterie in the small town of Semur-en-Brionnais, in the Saône-et-Loire department, almost in the middle of France. That's where I was born. The charcuterie belonged to my father: he made his living by peddling, on a market stall and in the shop, all the meats that he used to make, and my mother worked in the shop with him. One afternoon, while she was serving a farmer with black pudding, my mother felt me coming. She served the guy, closed the shop for the afternoon and telephoned the hospital: 'Come and fetch me!' My parents had a dog, a German Shepherd called Sultanne, who began to get very excited – she could tell that something was happening. And so my mother started to pack her little bag, a car arrived to take her to the hospital, and I was born that afternoon, on 8 October 1935.

1.  As a baby

Sometime later, I was brought back home to the flat above the shop. I was number two in the family, with a sister who was older than me by about sixteen months. So that was our family when I was born: my mother and father, my sister Liliane, and the dog. A photograph of me as a baby shows me perched on a velvet cushion, holding in my hands what looks like a pigeon: perhaps a prophecy of all the birds I would come to pluck in my future years. My brother Michel didn't come along until six years later, and my younger sister Martine arrived three years after that.

Semur-en-Brionnais used to be a market town, well known among those who love historical buildings for its beautiful twelfth-century church. It is a unique national monument: pale yellow stone with an octagonal tower, set among the pointed red mediaeval roofs of the main square. It was very rural. My father used to have his stall in the local market, and sell black pudding, garlic sausage, jambon, bourguignon, all of it made by him in that little shop. I vividly remember it; a typical Burgundy sausage shop, where you make the sausages and hang them up to dry and then bring them down when they are starting to flourish, and you see the surface beginning to mould and go white. Many years later – about forty years ago – I visited Semur. It hadn't changed – the church was still there, as was the bakery, the pottery, everything. Above all our shop was exactly as it had been left: pristine. It was closed, obviously, but the serving tables, the shelves, everything which was there before the Second World War were still in place. Even the name above the door: Charcuterie Roux. Nothing had been touched.

We lived in that small village until I was about five, when we had to move because of the war. We packed up our things – we didn't have a lot, just the basics – and travelled by bus to Charolles, a medium-sized town in Saône-et-Loire, where my grandfather had the charcuterie. The shop was right in the centre of the town, in the Place de l'Église. The flat on the third floor above the shop became our new home. That is, if you could call it a flat. It was tiny: just one room and a little kitchenette. I could look out from the window and see the handsome church opposite, and the other shops round the market square. We were way at the top, under the eaves, and my grandfather – my grandmother had died some years before – lived in the flat below. The smells of the charcuterie would permeate our flat; even our clothes smelt of it.

My grandfather had taken over the charcuterie shop from his father, who had started it. He was a well-known figure in the town, wealthy and very popular, and a good craftsman. He was also extremely mean with money. That's why he was rich. On market days the peasants would queue for his pâté and his saucisson and black pudding. It was a small, glass-fronted shop and very busy – his own little empire that he had built from scratch. And he had another shop elsewhere which he used mostly to dry his sausages – hundreds of them hanging up there, together with the ham. I was in awe of my grandfather and trembled when I saw him.

He was a hard-working man. On Tuesdays he would make the black pudding. I didn't get involved with killing the pig – my task was only to cut the onions for the black pudding – but I went a couple of times to see it killed. There my father would be with a big, long stick with a ball made of laurel wood at the end. They would cut the branches of this tree and use the end to make a mace, a solid thing like a hammer, which they used to kill the pig. My father would lure the pig into a room, tease him with scraps, and then bang! The pig would squeal and my father would plunge onto the poor beast with a sharp knife to cut its throat, catching the blood as he did so. My job would be to keep agitating the blood with some vinegar to make sure it didn't clot and curdle, so that it was ready for the black pudding. As soon as all the blood had finished flowing, my father would open up the pig to release the guts – the liver, the heart, the bladder. With a pig, everything can be eaten. It would then be taken outside, scorched on a bed of straw and shaved. After it had been shaved and washed they would bring the pig inside on a long wooden table where my father would butcher it: each part according to its eventual use. The legs would be put in brine to make jambon, the trotters would be kept separate to be sold. Even the tail was sold to make a delicious gelatinous dish.

The belly was used in a particular way: a typical Charolais urn, made from the clay which was abundant in the area, would be filled up a layer at a time: first a layer of sea salt then a layer of pork and so on, to make what we call *petit salé*. After a few months they would turn it, and the end product would finish up as a dish on the table – one that was very much prized by people in that part of the world. It is still a great favourite of mine. We used to eat it with cabbage when it was in season. The whole thing – killing the pig and butchering it – would take a day. If he was killing the pig on behalf of a

2. With my father and sister

farmer, my father would take one piece for himself from the animal. That's how he was paid, in kind.

Market day was once a week on a Wednesday and was a very important day for the town. Hundreds of peasants would arrive from all over the area, gathering in the Place de l'Église with their cream, their butter, their cheese, their saucissons. There would be live chickens and live rabbits for sale. All the payments were made in cash. I always found it absolutely fascinating. They would come in their traditional outfits – the women in long coloured skirts and aprons with shawls and white caps. There was a separate market for the beef, held down the road, where they would sell horses, as well as the beautiful cream-coloured Charolais cattle typical of the area. The peasants would bring their mares in to meet a stallion there, leading them into the *manège* to be seen to. I remember running down to have a look at it. It used to intrigue me: the size of the stallion and his long thing, how willing the mare was.

When I was very young I did not understand why my mother felt so miserable, but I grew to understand. He was a bit of a womaniser, my father, which caused my mother a lot of suffering. Although at heart he was a kind person, he had no idea how to treat the mother of his children. It was natural to him to misbehave, there was nothing faithful in his nature. It was not a happy marriage at all and she gave him his marching orders on several occasions. We children would be brought in as witnesses; she would call us in front of him and say, 'I hope you agree with this.' He was a big-hearted man, but he would not behave as he ought. As a father, he was not exactly neglectful, but he was not a father figure role model either. He showed his care for us in his own way. Many years later I was in the army in Algeria, and he had been told to disappear somewhere, so was living in the mountains in France. He wasn't earning that much, but he used to manage each month to put by a little money to send to me. I never asked him for it, but he sent it anyway. He had that sort of kindness.

When I was five I started school in Charolles. My mother took me on my first day. It was only a five-minute walk: past the river, then up the hill until we got to the school on the right-hand side. The weather was awful on that first day. My mother led me up the stairs. And then there I was, in a big room with all the other little boys and girls. It was what I would call a communal school: we were not separated into grades; instead the teachers would teach two or three classes at the same time in the same room. I don't know how they managed all the different syllabuses; there were about thirty children in the class, running from nursery school age, about six, to the age of fourteen when you had to pass the Certificat d'études. It was very old-fashioned, with a big stove keeping us all warm. We were given hot milk, and taught about our nice Marshal Pétain. We learned a song, '*Marechal, nous voila*' to sing every morning in honour of the general. That song is still with me, word for word. And then school started. Although it wasn't a Catholic school, we were taught to venerate Christ. We said a prayer every morning before launching into learning the alphabet; the school was – as were all schools in France since the revolution – cut off from the Church, though not entirely.

That first winter in Charolles was a bitter one. Food was scarce: we were short of butter, eggs, everything, because of the war. We had to feed the German army, more than two million soldiers, so the French got the leftovers. There was a thriving black market, because in those conditions there are always people who are out to make a profit. The black marketeers didn't care who they were selling to – Germans, French, it didn't matter to them. It went on twenty-four hours a day, every day, all the time. They sold any commodities they could get, and then there was a black market for the rationing coupons themselves. People with large families, like us, were always targeted because we had lots of coupons, for butter, sugar, eggs. My mother used to sell the coupons to make some much-needed money, but it meant we got less of everything to put on our own table. During the days with no school – Thursday and Sunday – my sister and I used to walk down into the countryside and knock on farm doors to ask if they had any eggs, butter, milk, anything they could spare. We were quite successful with the farmers, who would see two little children begging for eggs and be as generous as they could. We would bring everything we got back home, ready for my mother to cook.

I'm a strong believer that you are what you eat: it may be a cliché but for me it is entirely true. I believe too that the first introduction of food comes from the belly of your mother when she is pregnant. And being fed by my mother from birth until I was around a year old was very important – that's when the bond between mother and child gets strongly reinforced. All in all, I think my love for food came from my mother. My

3. With my mother and sister during the war

poor mum – all the time she was scrubbing, working, trying to make things work. You couldn't wish for a better mother and we worshipped her. She was a wonderful cook: simple, but wonderful. She knew that without money, she could still plunder what was in the fields. Because it was wartime, what we had to eat was what the Germans didn't want. Mostly that was offal – the liver, the heart, the tail, the leftover bits and pieces of the chicken. My mother excelled herself with the giblets, which hardly anybody wanted, and with the feet. Anything edible, she could find some way to make delicious. She would make a wonderful risotto and put the chicken feet in it, all cleaned up. Oh, the taste of that! She had the kind of flair that could make even an old pair of shoes taste fantastic. Flavour for her was always more important than anything else.

My brother's favourite, later on, was beef heart – the Germans didn't like the heart so it was ours to take for ourselves. My mother would braise the dense, strong heart meat with carrots. It wasn't one of my favourites, but it is a very nice dish. I remember vividly coming in from school every day and the way that the smell in the staircase would alert me to what was for lunch – whether it was pancakes, or stew, or soup. It is remarkable to me that my mother conjured all this from her tiny kitchen. It had an old-fashioned cooker which burned wood and coal – though coal was sparse at the time – and had a water container on the side which would warm the water while you were cooking.

Everything my mother cooked was very simple – it was cheap food but it was full of flavour. She was the queen of pancakes, which she used to serve with apples and pears that she had gathered in the autumn and preserved in jars in their own syrup. Like any French countrywoman she would always make jams and preserves, and did so throughout her whole life. I remember one Shrove Tuesday when we had brought back some eggs from our trip to the farms and had also managed to get a bag of flour. My father made some pancakes – they were his favourite thing to cook, too. Mother went to the cabinet and got out some *confiture* that she had preserved the winter before and I remember what a feast we had around those pancakes. They were a godsend. You could see the love in her face when she was putting it all on the table for us; at the end of the day, food is love.

As for me, I liked to observe my mother cooking. I tried a couple of times to help, but I was dismissed from the kitchen. She would say that I was too messy. Looking back, she was quite right.

Our town was in Free France – Vichy France – but it was very close to the demarcation line which divided us from occupied France, and the Germans would come to the town because of its size: it was a *sous-préfecture*. I remember seeing the Germans when they entered the town in their uniforms, the grey Wehrmacht and the black SS. I will never forget the ferocity of their barking German shepherds, pulling and straining on their leashes. As a whole, the town was divided: many of us hated the collaborators, but there were also the Milice, French paramilitaries who were pro-Vichy. I remember their uniforms as well: khaki. They were collaborators, a by-product of the German invasion.

*Childhood*

To me, as a child, the German soldiers did not really seem like humans – they were merely the enemy. Where we lived, in the building that belonged to my grandad, there were two shops – my family's charcutier and also a general store. One morning I went down to the shop to buy something for my mother. Two German soldiers arrived asking for '*Konfitüren!*' They wanted *confiture* – jam – of course. 'Haven't got any,' said the shop manager, but the soldier just became more and more vocal, angrily pointing at a pot of *moutarde de dijon* on the shelf. Losing patience, he grabbed the jar, opened it, put his finger in and started to lick it. '*Scheisse!*' he shouted, slammed the jar back on the shelf and marched out. '*Scheisse!*'

Charolles was not far from Paray-le-Monial, and on the main route between the larger cities of Montceau-les-Mines and Lyon, so there was a great deal of German traffic through the town. One evening there was a big bang and a lot of shouting in German. Looking outside, being careful not to be seen, I saw that a German motorbike and sidecar had entered the bakery round the corner from where we lived. It had missed the turn and run straight into the bakery – which luckily was closed – and the motorbike had caught fire.

Much worse, I recall the noise in the night when the Milice came to break down doors and arrest the Jewish people of the town. These were people we knew, these were the houses of our friends from school. The next day at school we would ask 'Where are your father and mother?' But there wouldn't be an answer. They were gone: arrested and sent to Ravensbrück and beyond, never to be seen again.

It was around the age of seven or eight that my fascination

for church and all the rituals that went with it began – it was like a magnet to me. My mother used to go to church, but she was not overly religious. We used to go every Sunday to the early service. I became an altar boy and would serve Mass every week. The first Mass was around seven o'clock and we were not allowed to drink or eat anything beforehand as communion could not be taken on a full stomach. I learned to administer the wine to the Father, and being a naughty boy I learned also to taste it, and add some water to it so he couldn't see that we had been at the bottle. Little did we know that he, of course, was fully aware of what we were doing.

There would be two services on Sunday morning, and then Vespers at about three o'clock in the afternoon. Afterwards we would be given 5 francs to go to the cinema in the town hall. We would leave the cinema at five thirty or six, walk home, have a bowl of soup and get into bed. There was a lady who used to look after all the choirboys: Mme Guichard. She used to come with her bicycle, and while we were walking to the cinema she would follow along behind us. One day, during a hard winter, her knickers fell down, right around her ankles. You can imagine the young boys, laughing their heads off. I will always remember her reaction: 'Don't worry, children,' she said cheerfully, 'I always wear two pairs.' She picked up her knickers, put them in her bag, and off we went.

I was always very close to my brother Michel throughout my life, but I remember little of him from when I was very young. He was so much smaller than me and a bit of a pain in the neck. We lived in such a tiny place that we were always on top of each other, and as the youngest he got all the attention.

At the table at dinner or lunchtime he would gobble his food like a little pig so that he would be first to get some more, and he would not hesitate to try and pinch food from my plate. He was – at that time – a bit of a so-and-so. But he was always precious to me and, as he got older, we became close. Later, once he got to school age, if he ever got into a fight with a bigger boy, he would refer the confrontation to me. All the classes came together at recreation, and if Michel thought he couldn't manage a situation, he would call me over and ask me to deal with it for him.

In the early days of the Second World War, my father had been made a prisoner of war. When the armistice between France and Germany was signed and the demarcation line was established, the prisoners from the Free France side of the border were liberated and my father was able to come back to Charolles. But as the war progressed, he joined the Resistance, doing a few little things and eventually entering the woods to fight. When I was about eight, our family moved to Prizy, a tiny town of just fifty people. Nobody knew where we were; we had gone incognito. It was really just a *hameau*, a hamlet – a collection of three or four households set in the flattish countryside, with an old church and a school and a few houses in the fields beyond. We moved into an empty house which belonged to a local farmer and stayed there for many months. It was surrounded by several grazing fields for finishing the beef before it went off to the abattoir. I have happy memories of that time: I made friends with the local farmers' sons and daughters and we did a lot of *vendange*: cutting the hay, spreading it out to dry, gathering it, taking it to the stable, piling it up for winter. We played with the cows that gave us milk, even climbing on their backs as they lay in the fields. But of course my father was not there much. We would see him sometimes at night, when he would come to the house in the dark and sit down for a bowl of soup and his regular couple of glasses of wine – he had not given up his habits! But otherwise, he lived in the forest. It was a dangerous time, though he was not to my knowledge tremendously active in the *maquis*, as the Resistance were known, and merely dabbled. He did not, however, like the Germans at all. And he venerated Stalin. There was a photograph of Stalin on the wall of our kitchen in Charolles. Of the two factions in the French Resistance; the Communists, and France Libre, my father was definitely a strong believer on the communist side.

After our months in Prizy, we moved back to Charolles. One morning when we arrived at school there were six empty chairs. These were the chairs of the children whose fathers had been picked up and executed in front of the church for Resistance activity. They had been told that there was a small contingent of Germans coming in on the main road that ran from Paray-le-Monial to Lyons – to get to Lyons you had to go through Charolles. The Resistance thought they could ambush the soldiers just before they reached the town and kill them. Unfortunately, just beforehand another contingent had been passing along the same road on their way to Germany. The Resistance opened fire, there was a fight, and the Resistance group lost. Two or three men were killed there: the others were arrested and six, seven or eight of them were executed in the Place de l'Église the next day. You can still

4. In Prizy, with my sister

find the graves of these victims of war in the main cemetery in Charolles: their tombs are marked by a black flag and the date they were shot by the Germans.

One famous evening American tanks and armoured vehicles drove into the town. Liberation! We all came out in our droves with our French flags, and went round the town hand in hand, singing and shouting. In the square I went up to one of our liberators, a tall American soldier. I took him by the hand and explained to him in French – though he couldn't speak a word of French of course, nor I English – that I wanted him to come with me and meet my mother. I brought him up to the third floor above the charcutier, my mother made him a coffee and he started to empty his pockets of chewing gum and Orangina and corned beef and peppermints. He stayed for about an hour, then off he went, back to his quarters.

The town was surprised to see the soldiers arriving, and even more surprised that they were American. We were expecting the English. In fact the troops that arrived were a mixture of American and our French-Canadian cousins. They stayed there for a week, and off they went, leaving behind a squadron of soldiers to guard the town. Because we were near the Ardennes, we never felt safe while the war was still going: the Germans were not far away. We always felt it, the apprehension that we would see the Wehrmacht marching back into town again. But they never did.

After that came the reprisals, when everyone suddenly became a *maquisard – de la dernière minute –* chasing anyone they thought had collaborated with the Germans. Chiefly they were after the women who had collaborated – they had been the queens of the town, always coming and going with the German officers, and they were fierce. But now the town had decided that the time had come for them to be brought down. From the window of my room on the third floor, I could see the hairdresser on the opposite side of the street. That's where they gathered these women – there were five or six of them – one morning. They put them outside naked in the bitter cold and shaved them – the hair on their heads, their pubic hair, the lot. Then they brushed them with tar and rolled them in feathers before marching them around the town with their hands on their head while people threw tomatoes or whatever was to hand. I saw all this, but I did not at the time comprehend why it was happening. All I knew was that people thought they had been naughty: they had had German lovers, and people thought they should be punished for it. After that the women were sent to the countryside for a while so that their hair could grow back. It was a long process, and it was perhaps six or eight months before they could end their exile and go back to normality, if they ever really did.

It was another bitter winter that year. I remember how bitter because of something which I thought was magical as a child; on the way to school the huge mound of gravel used to grit the icy road, was alight. The flames were leaping up into the sky and it felt to me like witchcraft. Of course there was a simple explanation: the soldiers had poured petrol on the mound and lit it to warm their hands.

During the war, I had seen Marshal Pétain on several occasions as he drove through the town. He would be riding in the back of the car, surrounded by a motorcycle escort, and he would wave as he went through. He must have been at least eighty years old at that point. I remember his marshal's hat with the gold braid. In the song we sang at school, Pétain is the 'Sauveur de la France'. But history tells a different story. In my view, he did collaborate, but he did so to try to save what was left after the defeat. There wasn't much choice involved. He was already an old man, past his eightieth birthday when he was chosen for the job, having been the French ambassador to Spain. He may not have done the right thing during the Occupation, but it seems wrong to ignore what he did for France in the First World War. He had been a hero: the hero of Verdun. His last wish was to be buried there, in the field. After the war he was condemned to death, and de Gaulle – who had been his protégé – commuted the sentence and imprisoned him instead on the Île d'Yeu where he ended his days. He died in peace, by himself, on that little island, and was buried there. I found it sad as a child. No more songs praising his glory. A new photograph went up on the wall at school: out with Pétain, in with de Gaulle.

I strongly believe that in France everyone at some stage became Gaulliste and at some stage became anti-Gaulliste – my father was no different. During the 1944 elections he sat glued to the static hiss coming from the old wireless, with a bottle of Beaujolais at his side. As the results from one town after another came in and it became clear a communist was to be elected, my father shouted 'Hooray' at the top of his voice. At the time, 40 per cent of the French voted for the communists and we had communists in the government, brought in by de Gaulle. They were ejected when he found out that Tillon, the air minister, was spying on behalf of Joseph Stalin. Tillon was disposed of and so were all the other communists.

~

After the war, my father struggled to find work in our little town and so he began to look for employment as a charcutier in Paris. My grandfather had moved to Paray-le-Monial to be looked after by one of his daughters, where he died a little while later. The shop had been sold to one of his employees, and my father was working at the time as a woodman. Eventually he found a job in Paris, which came with accommodation, and off we went as a family. It was a bit of a shock, a shock that started when we took a bus to Paray-le-Monial where the big train station was. We got onto the train and after it had been going for maybe an hour, it suddenly stopped. Everyone had to take their bags, get off the train and walk. We walked along a bridge which had been half destroyed to where another train was sitting on the tracks, waiting to take us to Paris.

We ended up in the district of Saint-Mandé. It had the typical streetscape of Paris – tall stone buildings with iron balconies lining the boulevards – but it was a suburb really. Our apartment was on the first floor, on a back street. It was very different from what I was used to; I had never been in a large town. Here there were no cows, no horses, just pavements and cars. It was a culture shock for me to see traffic, to witness all of these people going about their business, commuting to school and work. I had come from a tranquil place and suddenly it felt like I was in the jungle.

Psychologically, Paris was a city still emerging from the war. Physically, it had not been too damaged, although it was certainly traumatised. The city had been saved by General von Choltitz. Hitler gave his order: 'Burn it to cinders. Evacuate, but before you evacuate, burn it. Raze it to the ground!' But von Choltitz refused to oblige.

When we arrived, the city was in recovery. There was rationing for a couple of years after the war, but then the ration books went onto the fire, and things started appearing back in the shops. And if something was unavailable on the free market, you could still find it elsewhere if you had the money. I remember going to the *marché aux puces*, the flea market, where people were running the black market. You could get Camembert, butter or whatever you needed in the alleyways. Most of the Camembert had no fat in it – it was dry as a dodo – but it was still a Camembert, made the proper way. If you wanted the real stuff, the good stuff, it was there too, but you had to pay a bit more.

I went to the local school. It was a big school with all the classes separated by age. That was also new to me – in Charolles we had all learned together. Attached to the school was a huge barracks full of American army tanks, lorries and cars. One day as I was going into school the door opened up to let some vehicle come out and in the yard I saw two corpses hanging. They were soldiers who I assumed had been found guilty of some crime and executed. It was not the first time I saw a dead body, but it was the first time I saw somebody hanging on a string in the yard so all the others could see what happened if you misbehaved.

The accommodation my father had found was not large; there were only two main rooms. It was all very confined and once again my mother had a tiny kitchen to work in. The sink was a slab of stone with a cold water tap and a minuscule tank for hot water. Then there was a very small stove and that was it. It was very rudimentary. The bathroom was about the size of the toilet itself, and there was no bath or shower – you had to wash in the basin. There was one bedroom and then the main living room made up the rest of the flat – a couch, a wooden chest and a wooden dining table that was always covered in plastic. It always seemed dark in there because the shutters were usually closed against the noise of the street.

The thing I remember most about that flat was the smell of furniture polish. There were wooden banisters and creaky wooden floors throughout the building, we had no lift. The concierge was in charge of polishing all the wood and the smell infused the whole place; everything was incredibly shiny and slippery and smelling of beautiful beeswax.

Our flat had wooden floors too and my mother would keep them shiny with these polishing skates that she wore like slippers. She was very particular about housekeeping and everything was polished and tidy and very clean. What I didn't know when I arrived was that living on the sixth floor of that building was the girl who would later become my wife. But that was many years in the future.

Soon after we settled into that small flat my poor mother found herself pregnant again, with my sister Martine. The flat was far too small to accommodate five people, let alone six, so my mother's brother Paul and his wife Jeanne, who adored me as I adored her, offered to take me on. My aunt was greatly loved by my mother – they were the same age – and was happy to let me move in with them. I stayed there for two and a half years. Although it was small, they had a nice flat: two bedrooms, one dining room, one kitchen. And they had a dog, a papillon, called Bulbul who I quickly fell in love with. They had very big hearts, my aunt and uncle, and as they had no children of their own, I was treated as their child.

They lived in Ménilmontant, near Vincennes, an arrondissement right on the outskirts of Paris. From Ménilmontant, which is high on a hill, you overlook Paris – from some streets you can see the Tour d'Eiffel. There is even a vineyard up there. My uncle was a shoemaker and spent his days making and repairing shoes. I had a very happy time there, though unfortunately my aunt was always 'between two drinks', and she and my uncle used to fight like dog and cat. We would go to see my family in their flat in Paris, with my aunt half drunk. When she entered the building she used to call out in a groan, 'Mermaine! Mermaine!' (my mother's name was Germaine). 'Calm down, Jeanne, calm down,' my mother would say. What struck me, even as a child, was that my uncle would never say, 'Auntie Jeanne has been drinking.' He would say, 'Auntie Jeanne is not well, you have to excuse her.' But oh, how they would fight – often with fists, sometimes with plates. Bulbul and I would finish up quite often under the bed together to avoid the flying shoes and dishes. Poor little Bulbul would be trembling.

The drinking wasn't the only problem. My aunt was one of twenty-two children and was a very strong woman. She was also very beautiful, and extremely promiscuous. My uncle knew all too well what she was up to, especially in the country. They had a little house in Normandy where we would go and spend the summer holiday. And it seemed as though all the men in the village would queue up to visit my aunt. I was old enough to understand what they were up to: I would see it with my own eyes, and hear it too. Afterwards I would knock at the window and say, 'Hey! What about me, I'm here!' and the man would hop out of bed totally naked, quickly pull his trousers on and go running to the larder where there was a tiny window. Goodness knows how they used to wriggle out of that window, but they would all disappear that way. My aunt would jump out of bed saying, 'Oh, hello, I was just asleep.' I'm sure. They were all at it – the farmers and even, which seemed to me particularly strange, my other uncle, Ernest, who was the brother of her husband.

I was still very religious and interested in the church at that time. When I was twelve I had taken my first communion, smartly dressed up in a suit with my bible and rosary, white gloves and communion ribbon. It felt as though the church was my destiny. One of the first things I did when I came to Ménilmontant was to find the local church and enrol myself. The idea, still fermenting in my mind, was for me to eventually become a priest. I met with the *curé* who was in charge there. He was not an impressive figure. He seemed to me to be very old – though he must have only been around sixty – and he always had traces of his breakfast on his robes. Above all, he smelled; the chief thing I remember about that old man was the smell that emanated from his clothing.

The *curé* had the idea that another altar boy and I should both learn Latin; it was a requirement for the priesthood as in those days Mass was said in Latin. He used to give private lessons. Oh, private they were. It turned out that these so-called lessons were totally for his own benefit. The first thing he did was to undo my trousers and manipulate my testicles. I thought it was quite strange and I started to doubt that it had anything to do with me wanting to be a priest. He did it twice. After the second time, the other guy – I remember he was the same age as me, but taller – was waiting outside for his turn when I finished my lesson. As I came out of my second session, I asked him, 'What does he do to you? Does he take your trousers off?'

'Oh yes!' he said.

'Well, I'm not going back in there,' I said to myself. 'That is not normal.'

I never said a word to the priest again. I just didn't turn up. He had been doing that for years, I suppose. And of course he was not the only priest to behave like that.

So that was the end for me and the Church. I closed the book and I never talked to my mother, and certainly not my father, about what had happened. Before long I started to blame myself. In fact, it took a good fifteen or twenty years for me to realise that I was not the culprit in that situation. I still very much believed in God, but I just couldn't go to Mass anymore. I never confided to anybody, not even my first wife, as to why I was so reluctant to set foot in a church.

When I got married, many years later, the ceremony took place in a church because I wanted the children to be

5. Dressed up for holy communion

baptised as Catholics. The priest in Tonbridge – where the Catholic church was – was a dear man. I think that might have triggered me starting to question the reasons why I was cutting myself off from the church. I did reconcile myself to the Catholic faith eventually – it took twenty-five years for me to go back, and it came about because of the Queen of Romania and her wonderful charity. But that is another story for later.

After two years living with my aunt and uncle I went back to my own family. But in truth this was a sombre time for me, because I was approaching my fourteenth birthday, and it was time to leave school and start my apprenticeship.

# 2

## Apprenticeship

My father would have loved for me to be a charcutier. Four generations of our family had done that job. But it never appealed to me: it's wet, it's cold, it's not me. The smell of the pork intestine gets into your skin and takes days to wash off. You can wash your hands, wear clean clothes; whatever you do, you will still smell it. What I wanted was to be a cook. At school, when I announced this, there was laughter from the kids, and then a great silence. To them, it was funny. They thought that cooking wasn't a natural job for a man. But I took their laughter in my stride. In my head, being a cook would ensure that I was well fed every day. That was definitely uppermost in my mind, and having abandoned the idea of becoming a priest, food was my second love. So whatever my classmates thought, to me cooking was quite a natural destination.

It was the *smell* of cooking that first attracted me: that may

29

sound funny, but it is a fact. The smell, and the garden. To be able to go out into the garden and pick the carrots, the French beans, peel them, clean them, cook them and eat them, taking the process from the very beginning to the end. That felt like something worthwhile. I've always felt close to the land, to the farmer, where it all starts. It's not anything anybody has taught me; it's just how I am. It is why I love animals, and nature. We have a marvellous world, which unfortunately quite a few people abuse. But we're fighting to redress it and we will succeed.

The next question was how to get started, now that I was leaving school. My father happened to know the chef to the Duchess of Windsor, Monsieur le Pellequier, from having worked at one time with his nephew. So we paid him a visit. His advice was clear: 'Before being a chef, you have to be a good *pâtissier*: it is the most useful thing you can do. Do your apprenticeship in that. Then in three years' time, when you have finished your apprenticeship, come back to me and I will be sure to find you a job in a kitchen.' Actually, I did not really want to be a *pâtissier*, but he was a top Parisian chef so I took his advice. He was probably right, too. Pastry is very much a science and it teaches you a particular discipline – how to properly read and follow a recipe. In the rest of the kitchen things can be a little more free-flowing and down to taste, but not in pastry. For pastry, you need exact accuracy. Then, once you have learnt to be precise, you can go and work in the kitchen as a chef. If you do it the other way round, that precision is very hard to instil.

To start me off on this new career, my father took me to the

Society of Bakery, St Michel. They had a little office near Place de la Concorde, and every day at four o'clock, religiously, they would call out the available jobs in *pâtisseries* and boulangeries all over Paris. They said they happened to have an opening for an apprentice in one of the local *pâtisseries* in St Mandé, close to where we lived, called Maison E. LeClerc. So we made an appointment, my father presented me to Monsieur LeClerc, and I got a job in his *pâtisserie*, a three-year apprenticeship. Monsieur LeClerc was very tough. He had been imprisoned by the Germans during the war for four years, and when he got out he bought that little shop, which became very successful. He was married to an Austrian woman. She barely spoke French, but she was charming.

Physically, the job was hard. For the apprentice, there were great big bags of flour and sugar to hump around. In those days the maximum weight bag was much bigger than it is now: 25 kg, compared to 10 kg nowadays. It was a lot to carry, and that was only one of the menial and tedious tasks.

I would start working at 7 a.m. The first task of the morning was to break the eggs for the first batch. You would crack them open, sniff them to make sure they had not been laid two months before – it did happen – and only then add them to the basin. If you put the eggs straight into a basin with thirty-two others, one bad egg will ensure the whole bloody lot is bad. On top of that, every time you crack an egg, you have to make sure that it is totally clean by sweeping it out with your thumb so that every drop of the white ends up in the pastry. You crack each egg, you smell it, then you clean it. Over and over, because there are hundreds and hundreds

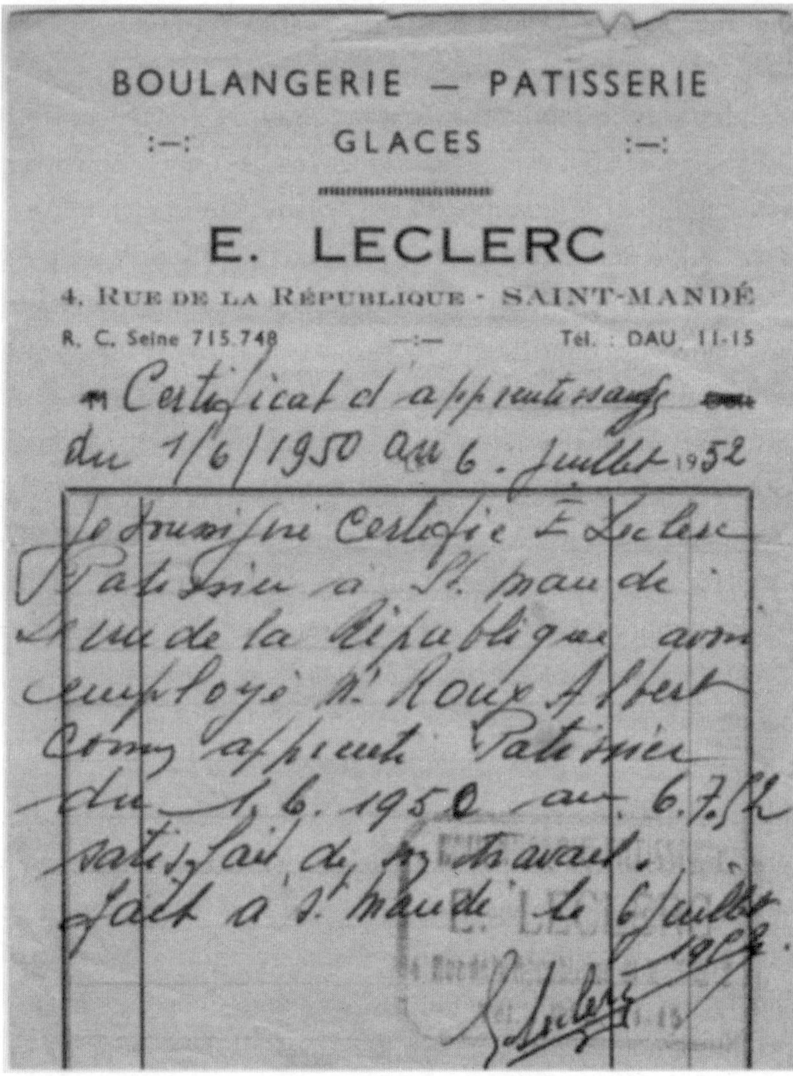

BOULANGERIE — PATISSERIE

:—: GLACES :—:

E. LECLERC

4, Rue de la République - SAINT-MANDÉ

R. C. Seine 715.748 —:— Tél. : DAU 11-15

Certificat d'apprentissage
du 1/6/1950 au 6. Juillet 1952

Je soussigné Certifie E. Leclerc
Patissier à St Mandé
Rue de la République avoir
employé M. Roux Albert
Comme apprenti Patissier
du 1. 6. 1950 au 6.7.52
satisfait de son travail.
Fait à St Mandé le 6 Juillet
1952.

6. Apprenticeship certificate

of eggs to crack in a day. Nowadays it's different – you're not allowed to do that. Instead you buy in liquid yolk, liquid white, pasteurised whole egg, and the recipes all rely on weights rather than numbers. There's no counting any more.

All of this took a long time to learn. A first-year apprentice wouldn't be trusted even to count the eggs. Your job was to crack them, with guidance at first, but not count them. You weren't allowed to weigh other ingredients out, not for the first few months at least. But you would peel ten crates of pears and cook them down. For the pain au chocolat, you might be allowed to take the chocolate and put it in the dough, and maybe fold it over, hundreds of times a day. But making the dough and handling it – no, not at first.

You repeated these very, very basic jobs constantly until they became second nature. And then you became quick at it. Take lining tart moulds: there's a certain way. You only get fast with practice. We would make the general pastry for the day; the croissants, the brioches, eclairs, religieuses. Then there were all the festivities that the French celebrate: the galette that was extremely popular where you put a little boy or girl figurine inside. If you finish up with it, you are king or queen for the evening. It's a ritual. There were different pastries for all sorts of occasions.

Then you would have all the cleaning. There was an incredible amount to be done: all the racks, all the trays, all the ovens. Nowadays you have ovens that you can programme for different heats and different humidities. Back then, there was just one type – solid brick, with racks. You'd have probably three going at three different temperatures, and if you wanted humidity you put a wet rag in there. Then you would have to clean the tart rings, the moulds, everything made completely pristine every day and the trays scraped down with rags. There would be sawdust on the floors, put down clean every day, and scrubbed every week, like you see in butchers and charcutiers.

The tiny little fidgety work of pastry-making came later, after you'd proved that you could clean and understand basic orders and be disciplined. It would take maybe a year before an apprentice would be able to make something from scratch and have it displayed in the shop window.

There was a lot of pleasure in the work for me. There is always a fantastic smell in a pastry shop. There are fresh blocks of yeast, and there is always dough fermenting. In the morning there's the aroma of leavened dough being cooked, and after that you have the sweetness of marzipan and pralines and almonds, and maybe later in the afternoon when it's a bit cooler there would be the strong smell of cocoa powder from any chocolate work.

So it was a good place for me, and I certainly wasn't unhappy there, but after two years, I found myself wanting to move on. I felt I had exhausted the possibilities there as far as learning was concerned. In those days, when you signed the apprenticeship contract you couldn't break it. You had to have the owner's permission. So I asked my father to write to Monsieur LeClerc and ask him to release me. My parents were not very keen on my moving, but I pursued it anyway. I was determined. I went back to the famous society at St Michel and explained to them that I had come to the end of the road at my current workplace, and my father wrote to Monsieur LeClerc. He wasn't very pleased at all, and I can understand why. When you take on an apprentice, the first year is expensive. The apprentice only really becomes useful in their last year, because by then they are doing the job of a commis chef, but they are only paid an apprentice's wages. So it would have been a blow to him. Nevertheless he reluctantly gave his consent, signed the paper, and I found a job in another pâtisserie called Aux Rois Mages.

Aux Rois Mages was a new shop which had opened in the high street in Vincennes, a different suburb of Paris. It was a busy shop, and a beautiful one, bright and warm and smelling of pastry. It was an absolutely typical French *pâtissier* – there were wonderful pastries in glass cabinets: croquembouches, croissants, brioches. The owner worked downstairs in the basement, making the pastry in what we called the lab. He too was married to a foreigner – a German woman whom he had met while he was a prisoner of war in Germany. He spoke German to her because she could not speak French, but somehow she still managed to run the shop. When she couldn't understand what the customers needed, she would come downstairs to the corner where the boss would be snatching some sleep on a little mattress in between baking. She would go and wake him up with her foot to come upstairs and be the interpreter. As a German in post-war Paris, she was not always made to feel welcome by the customers. But it worked between them, somehow: love is marvellous.

I spent the whole day every day downstairs with the owner. At that stage I still wouldn't have been allowed to serve in the shop. My place was in the basement with the dough and the eggs and the flour and sugar. I was there from seven in the morning till four thirty in the afternoon. It suited me beautifully: it was not wet and it was not cold – it was kept wonderfully warm by the heat of the oven. Quite unusually for the time, in Aux Rois Mages the boss used to do absolutely everything himself. We used to make our own marzipan and our own fondant rather than buying it in: we would get rough almonds, in their skin, and clean them up – peel them, take the skin off by hand, chop them into a paste, mix them with sugar. You name it, he did it. He was a real artisan. His goal was perfection, and he had a good name. The shop was new, but it didn't take long for his customer base to build up.

Paris in those days was exciting. At that point the division between the haves and have-nots was wide. Very wide. So there were a lot of people living with next to nothing, and on the other hand people living quite opulent lives because they had cash. The customers in the shop were petit bourgeois, well to do, well dressed and content. They weren't carrying any marks from the war. As for me, it was a terrific time. I had plenty to eat, plenty of cakes. But it wasn't an easy life. You worked, you went home, you washed, went to bed, got up in the morning, washed, went to work . . . As for weekends – they started at about three o'clock in the afternoon on Sunday, after you'd worked around the clock since Friday. Saturday and Sunday were the busy days. In that long long shift the only rest you got was leaning on a bag of flour or corn and trying to get an hour's sleep. That was the life.

My father, to all intents and purposes, had disappeared by

PATISSERIE - CONFISERIE
"AUX ROIS MAGES"
116 bis, Cours de Vincennes
DOR. 46-47 — R. C. Seine 1.442.206

Paris, 3. 11. 52

Je certifie avoir eu à mon service comme patissier

Albert Ronse

du 1. 9. 52 jusqu'à ce jour.

Pendant ce temps je n'ai eu qu'à me louer de ses services me quitte ce jour libre de tout engagement.

PATISSERIE - CONFISERIE
"AUX ROIS MAGES"
116 bis, Cours de Vincennes
DOR. 46-47 — R. C. Seine 1.442.206

**7. Apprenticeship certificate**

this time. He left the flat in Paris and got a job as a charcutier somewhere in the country. I never really knew where exactly he had gone, and I never saw him again. It was rather sad. He gave me his watch at some point before he left, though I am afraid it got lost in Africa. So now, it was once again my mother who kept the family alive, looking after my brother and little sister. My older sister had by this time got a job in the local charcuterie, and had taken on the role of the master of the house. I was not fond of her, I am afraid. It felt to me then as if she had taken over. At the table, if I wanted something more to drink, I had to ask my sister's permission. Just for a glass of water! And often she would say, 'You've had enough.' There was a dictatorial side to her that I could not stand.

All in all, life was good. The craft of the *pâtissier* was not really for me, though, in the end: it is too precise. Pastry equals chemistry. You have your pastry book, you have your recipe, but if you make a mistake on the amount of flour going into the cake, then that's it: it's hard as a rock. In other cooking, let's say your sauce is too salty, you can adjust it. So there's more freedom. But Monsieur le Pellequier was right: it is certainly good training for the craft. When my brother Michel was a young boy at school, they used to ask him, 'What do you want to do with your life?' His answer was, 'Whatever my brother does.' Bless him. So when, some years later, he decided he wanted to follow me into the trade, he too did a pâtisserie apprenticeship. Unlike me, he fell in love with it. He was an artist, and he enjoyed the detail of it all. That was his nature: his entire attitude to work was absolutely minute and precise. So pâtisserie suited him down to the ground. But for me, while I enjoyed the process of learning and the skills it brought, it was never the whole answer.

So the job wasn't perfect for me, but it suited me fine. The boss was an extremely good craftsman and a very hard worker. My philosophy has always been that in any job, you don't ask, 'What am I going to earn?' No, the thing to ask is, 'What am I going to learn for the future?' If you didn't ask, you would never know. Bosses didn't always make it easy to learn: in those days most of the time if you asked something you were told to go back to work and not waste time. But that boss was quite generous with his answers, and I learned a lot from him.

I didn't stay the full year in the end. Unfortunately, a little incident saw me out – it was the story of my life. I was found kissing one of the sales girls in the fridge. I was dismissed, to my great regret. So it was back to St Michel and the Society of Bakery. Every night I used to go and apply for whatever jobs were available, and finally one came up in a *biscuiterie*, a sort of semi-factory, making biscuits that were sold into supermarkets and shops.

Throughout this period I used to go and visit Monsieur le Pellequier every New Year; it's another ritual we have in France, to pay visits at New Year to show respect. It was a long long journey by metro from St Mandé to the Arc de Triomphe, where he lived. I used to hate doing it, but every year I would go and knock at the door with a bouquet of flowers tied up by my mum, looking like a weirdo, to wish him and his family a Happy New Year and try to make sure he would remember me in the future.

However much I hated the ordeal, it must have worked: after I had done my three years of apprenticeship, I went back to see Monsieur le Pellequier once more to give him his New Year good wishes and to ask him about jobs. To my great surprise, on this occasion he said, 'Yes, I do have a vacancy at the moment. It's in London.' There was a job available at Lady Nancy Astor's establishment. At that time, the name meant nothing to me. I knew of London from my geography lessons at school and not much else. And I couldn't speak a word of English. But I accepted. Although I didn't know it at that stage, the course of my career was suddenly about to become very interesting. That was all in the future though: first, I had to wait for the documents to be sorted out to be allowed to work in England. So there I was, working in the biscuit factory, anxiously waiting for my permit to come. Soon I would be in England, where my life would change.

# 3

## England

So this was to be the start of my new life.

I took a train to catch the ferry. On the train I met three typical upper-class English girls – you could tell from the way they were dressed – who I engaged in conversation. As yet I had no English at all, but they had pretty good French. It turned out that they were working at the British embassy in Paris. They asked why I was coming to England, and when I explained to them, they were excited to learn that I was going to work for the Astors. It was only then that I began to realise that my new employers were a well-known family. In particular they were impressed that I would be working for Lady Astor herself. She was a very impressive character, it seemed: at the forefront of society, the first woman to sit in parliament, the leading figure of a hugely wealthy family.

The crossing – my first journey by sea – was awful. Gale force winds made me sick as a dog. At last, we arrived in

Folkestone. Before disembarking I had to have a medical, and the doctor, who could speak a little bit of French, told me I was not looking good at all. 'Well,' I said, 'if you had a crossing like that, neither would you.' But he let me in, and there I was, in England. Off I went in the train, and finished up in Victoria station at around five thirty in the evening. It was winter, so it was dark. And suddenly from all sides came all these people, rushing. It was not raining that day, but they each had an umbrella, a carnation on their lapel, and some funny rounded hat on their head. I thought it was carnival time, and that this was a kind of costume. When the Astor's chef arrived at the station to pick me up I had to ask him about it. 'No,' he said, 'that is the normal uniform for people working in the City.' The bowler hat and the umbrella: welcome to London.

That was my first encounter with English tea, as well. He took me to a Lyons Tea Room, where to my great surprise the chef had to give us a rationing coupon for our food. In England, it seemed, people were still using coupons, which had long disappeared in France. This was 1953, years after the war. It was quite interesting to see that this country was still in its grip.

My first encounter with the Astors was the next day. I was told that Lady Astor wanted to meet me. I was shown the door where she would come into the kitchen to say hello, and reminded by the chef about how I should behave. The instruction was not to speak, not a word, until I was spoken to, and then only to answer questions. So a delegation from upstairs arrived, and at the head of them was that little lady, Lady Astor. She asked me a few questions, welcoming me into the house, and off they went out for dinner. She must have been in her seventies, but she was still forceful: a resolute presence.

After a short time I was transferred to the service of her son, John Jakie Astor, who was later the liberal MP for Plymouth. Lady Astor was going to America for a couple of months, so she lent me to him, so to speak. I was taken to Gamlingay– one of the Astor family estates, near Cambridge – a beautiful manor house made of red brick and stone, with acres of gardens and parkland. To my delight it also had a stud, because they were very keen owners of thoroughbreds.

At Gamlingay, I realised that there was another world than the one I was used to, and also that it was the sort of the world that I wanted to stay in. Even as a lowly helper in the kitchen, I had my own room, with my own bathroom. There was a whole roasted chicken put on the table twice a week: at home, that was something that we only got at Christmas. In normal times we only had the giblets. This was luxury indeed.

I was with the household for nearly a year. There were four of us in the kitchen. The chef was Italian: that is, he had a French passport but he was of Italian descent. I was the scullery boy. That was the official description on my permit. I had been trained as a pastry chef for three years; here, though, I was in a totally different world. It was October when I came, the shooting season. For my first job I was confronted with dozens and dozens of pigeons, pheasants, partridge, unplucked. They had come into the kitchen to be prepared. I was given a little seat and this huge huge pile of birds. What a job! You had to make sure you did not damage the skin, so you had to pluck them feather by feather. It was a nightmare. After the plucking, I moved on to drawing the birds, and trussing them with a piece of lard on top. They had to be prepared either to be eaten there, or to give to the guests on departure in a little box. It was a big shoot – about ten guns, so there were about three or four hundred pheasants. The smell of it all; dear oh dear.

This was the beginning of my education in the food of English private service. It started with how to cook breakfast, which was a grand affair. It was all laid out on the sideboard: kedgeree, kippers, you name it. Scrambled egg, fried egg, boiled egg. It was the epitome of English food; all the classics. Then there was lunch and high tea and dinner. At weekends, when there were guests, there would be grand dinners. The menus were planned out a week in advance: the chef would go up with his book to get his instructions and everything considered down to the last detail.

Famously I once got into trouble when the then prime minister, Harold Macmillan, was staying for the weekend, and I managed to get his *oeufs en cocotte* jammed in the dumb waiter. It was the first instance of my lifelong problems with dumb waiters.

The food during the week was often lighter: *bouillon de legumes*, sardines on toast, because the family would be on diets recuperating from heavy boozy weekends. There were also staff to be fed, and there was a woman whose job was to cook the staff food. She was a bloody good cook. Everything she cooked was extremely delicious, and from my perspective extremely plentiful. What struck me most was the abundance that there was on the table, coming from a place where food was not easy to get. There was still rationing in England, but the family had a farm of thousands of acres. There was no restriction in that kitchen on cream or on butter, and they would slaughter their own animals. All the food you wanted was there in plenty. I remember once in London the old lady, Nancy Astor, coming down to the kitchen to see the chef. When I say coming down, I mean rushing down, and bellyaching because they had run short of butter and cream. Oh la la, did she give it to him: 'Haven't we got a farm? Haven't we got cows and chickens?' Formidable woman! It was rare to see her in that kitchen – I had only encountered her in that first welcome when I arrived – we were downstairs, she was up. But when she was annoyed enough, she came down.

From that staff cook I learned how to make pies, Christmas pudding, stew: all the beautiful English dishes. What I would call dishes of comfort. Because English food is for comfort, in my view, far more than French food is. French food is for the pleasure of the palate. I'm not saying that English food is not delicious, but its overall purpose is comfort, and warmth. I had my little book, where I would note down all her recipes. It was a pleasure to add this cuisine to my repertoire. I loved learning these new dishes. French chefs, on the other hand, the ones I worked for in the UK, were very secretive. When asked questions, they said, 'Nothing to do with you.' They didn't want to divulge the way they did things, but I soon learned that you learn a lot through watching. So I observed.

As well as the chef and me in the kitchen, there was also

a commis chef and a cleaner. Then there were butlers and footmen, and there was an army of Spanish and Italian chambermaids, waitresses and what have you. There was no shortage of women, I remember that, and I was a young man away from home. That's when I found a watch came in very handy!

It was a nice kitchen, huge, with plenty of room for everybody. It had everything you would expect to have in that kind of household. The cooking was done on an Aga, a proper coal one that heated up the water at the same time. I thought it was marvellous – an Aga keeps you warm, it keeps the water warm. Keeping it going was the job of Paddy, the Irishman, who looked after all the fires in the place and introduced me to football. I became very friendly with him. He couldn't speak French, nor could I speak a word of English at first. But I made it my business to learn. I see this with the workforce even today, they don't make an effort to meet with the natives. I made it my aim to embrace their habits. I would go out with them to the local ballrooms, where I didn't take the dancefloor because I couldn't dance the dances – it's not for me, the quickstep and all of that. But I have to say I met some charming girls, who took it upon themselves to teach me English. And they were very good teachers, thank goodness.

It was also at Gamlingay that my love of horses really started. I remember sneaking down at night to the stud there, looking at those horses. They were so beautiful – and many of them were famous too. It's still very vivid in my mind, as vivid as the horses on market day back in Charolles.

8. In London

9. Relaxing in London in my time off

To me everything about this life was new, it was luxury. It was about the way you were treated as a servant – you were treated properly, dealt with fairly. That felt surprising to me, because at that time, in France, 40 per cent of the country embraced the communist party, and there was a huge amount of propaganda about the filthy rich people. So for me it was a new perspective: to discover that these people may be filthy rich, but long may that last! That was my view; if they are going to treat other people properly and look after them, then the more rich people the better.

I stayed in Gamlingay for the best part of three months, and then the household moved to London. John Jakie Astor had bought a very nice house in Knightsbridge, just opposite Harrods, and the chef and I operated from the kitchens there. London was still reeling in shock after the war – compared to Paris the physical destruction was still visible everywhere. I had a girlfriend in Elephant and Castle – I remember going to fetch her when we went out and the area down there was like a bombsite, because that specifically had been the place where most V1 and V2 rockets exploded. London had been crushed physically, but mentally not so much. There was a sense of opportunity, a feeling of possibility, that things could happen there, probably because it had never been under occupation as Paris had.

They were happy years. I met with nothing but kindness, and learned to understand what you might call the British way of life, because there is a British system. I welcomed that, and understood it much quicker than if I had kept myself to myself. When we were in London, I used to go to Hyde Park Corner to watch the speakers stand on their little stools, haranguing passers-by. I was intrigued to see that there were hardly any police present. I remember going back to the kitchen and describing the scene to the chef, amazed at how peaceful the scene was, and that nobody there was fighting. And he said, 'No. In this country they don't fight, they express themselves, and provided they don't say anything against royalty they are free to say any propaganda they like.'

To me, that really was freedom. Having seen my family fighting each other like cat and dog over politics, because my father was a communist, I knew I wanted to be a part of this society. It is true to say that this country is not as free in speech as it used to be, but it is still one of the most liberal countries that I have yet encountered. I think that's where the roots of my desire to stay and one day become a British citizen lay. And I'm pleased to say that now I am one. I was so proud to get my British passport, and to have been honoured by the Queen in receiving an OBE in 2002. I'm absolutely fascinated by the Queen, and fascinated too by the way the English address their politics. Take the shaking hands at the end of an election: the sentiment is, 'Well done my boy, I've lost but so what?' It may seem like hypocrisy at times, but there is something admirable in the way that it is all done so mildly. Witnessing all of this, I could only fall in love with the country and its people, and that love that I have has not diminished an inch over the years: far from it. My wish and desire is to be buried in this country. I have no thought of going back to live in France. I am converted: this is home.

After working for the Astors for a while I tried very hard

to get a permit to work in a restaurant over here. Even then, my ultimate aim was to have my own restaurant, so I wanted to gain experience of restaurant life. But it proved impossible to have my permit transferred, even after I lined up a job. I decided in the end to leave the Astors and seek another job in private service. I went through a company called the Macey Agency who specialised in private houses. They were there to supply butlers, chefs, washers up, cleaners: everything that was needed for the smooth running of a house. It was through them that a new job arrived, and I went to Ireland to work for a gentleman called Ambrose Congreve and his wife. You couldn't mistake him for anything but Irish, but of a very particular sort, the kind that came over with Cromwell. The house – Mount Congreve – was in Waterford. They were extremely wealthy, and it was a beautiful house, with a famous and fantastic garden. They used to spend a couple of months there every year. They were wonderful people, both of them. I can't speak too highly of them. They were Protestants themselves, but very conscious that most of the staff were of the Catholic faith. On Sundays after cooking breakfast they would send us all to Mass, chauffeur driven in a large car, with a picnic. They themselves would have a cold lunch and dinner.

Fate had it that many years later, when Ambrose Congreve discovered I had opened a restaurant and become famous, he invited me for dinner in his house in London. By then, his wife had died. It was an extraordinary evening. The house was No 1, next to St James's Palace. The service was absolutely impeccable, all staffed by Indian waiters, dressed in plumes and turbans. The food was delicious: I remember it was the grouse season at the time. There was a mixture of people there – about fourteen of us, and I took my wife with me. She was amazed by the wealth and the grandeur. At the end, the ladies got up, and when I stood up to follow them, the guy next to me – I can't remember who it was – said, 'No no. You don't get up. You stay put. The ladies retreat.' Which I thought was bizarre. I wanted to follow the women, but instead I had to stay behind with the boys, who started to talk about politics and tell naughty jokes. Ambrose Congreve kept asking me for dinner – I went back there three or four times, and when he published his memoir he dedicated a page and a half to me.

I stayed with the Congreves a good part of a year, and then one day one of the guests' drivers told me that his boss might want a chef; would I be interested in applying for a job? I thought that was rather strange – a guest trying to poach the chef. I found out afterwards it was widely done in that circle. The driver's boss was Charles Clore, a well-known figure in the financial world. He was a great entrepreneur, buying a lot of buildings, boat yards, Dolcis the shoe people; anything that he thought would make him money. He ended up owning Selfridges. It turned out he was indeed looking for a chef, so I left the Congreves and went to my new lodgings at 97 Park Street.

# 4

## Algeria

But all of this – my life in London – was about to be interrupted. Throughout the years I had been learning my trade and working away, a conflict was being fought hundreds of miles away. What was then part of France – Algeria – was in uprising, and the French government was calling up ever more young men to try and suppress it. I was in Great Britain when I was called up to the army. The papers were sent by the embassy: report to the camp at Maison Laffite. I was expecting this, but I didn't welcome it. I asked for a six-month delay, which because I was abroad was automatically granted, but I had no way to escape; the only way out would be to surrender my French passport and apply for a British one, which I was not prepared – or eligible – to do. So, short of eloping I couldn't avoid it: I was going to Algeria.

I had an interview and they felt I was the right fabric to be an officer: 'officer material', was how they put it. But after

10.  In uniform

some months of having me in the barracks, they decided a commission was not a good idea, and I agreed with them. You could say I was too controversial for them, too forward. I was twenty-one and I had already been working for about seven years. I had a tendency to ask too many questions.

Rather than transferring me into another regiment, they kept me where I was as a guardian of the chalet. So I stayed at Maison Laffite for three months. Those months were like a holiday camp – there was nothing much for me to do except for making sure the place was kept nice and clean. This wasn't too onerous: there were only about thirty guys there. I had to go and fetch any visitors who came to the barracks, and generally keep things in order.

All of this was easy enough, but there were other things to learn: how to dismantle a gun and put it back together. How to use a grenade. The first time they gave me a grenade – it was what they call an offensive grenade – they showed me how to pull the trigger, and as I pulled it I whipped around to watch them, only to find that they were running away as fast as they could, and taking shelter behind a wall. I looked down: I still had the grenade gripped in my hand. 'Throw it!' shouted the instructor. I threw it pretty hard.

It was quite an easy life. Michel came to visit me on my days off. We were able to have the odd day out together. But it couldn't last: after three months of this holiday camp life I was finally to be sent to Algeria. Tin hats on, and rucksacks packed, we boarded the train. I ended up in Marseilles, waiting for the boat for a couple of days. And then it was time: down a gangplank, onto the ship and off to Algeria.

11.  A day out with my brother

This was 1955–6, so it was still pretty early in the uprising. As recruits, we knew what was happening in Algeria, that it was in a state of rebellion. We knew also that every day there was a crime committed – that there were bombs and other incidents, and that there were further problems with the next-door neighbours – the Tunisians and Moroccans – so that we would be the defensive line. Part of our task would be to stop the rebels crossing the borders with ammunition and supplies. But we didn't perhaps understand the full picture.

On arriving in Algeria I was transported straight away to a train which took me to a place called Dellys, a little old-fashioned traditional Algerian town, on the coast about a hundred kilometres from Algiers. It was all very new to me – the palm trees, the inhabitants in their traditional dress. I found myself riding donkeys and watching camels race. At the barracks I was transferred into the officers' mess as a chef. My job was to cook for the officers – twenty of them. It involved everything from going shopping for the menus to cooking the food. I do remember it being so hot you could fry an egg on the bonnet of the tank.

It certainly felt a long way from home. I used to receive money from my father, even though it had been a long time since I had last seen him. And even better, my brother Michel was following in my footsteps by doing his apprenticeship at that time. On his days off he would cook cakes at home which he would pack up and send to me by post. They were often the worse for wear after their long journey, but they were very precious to me.

My posting in Dellys didn't last long; I was only there

12–14. The journey to Algeria

for about three months. It was too stuffy. I rebelled, again. I was always getting into scrapes over small things, like not wearing the proper uniform. I used to have a chicken in the kitchen, called Gertrude, who I had adopted, and who laid me eggs every day. That was until one day some idiot fed her cognac which killed her. So I lost Gertrude. Later on I got an Alsatian dog: a very devoted girl called Sultanne. She was very protective; nobody approached my bed without her trying to bite.

Because of the scrapes I got into I was transferred into disciplinary company. It was within the same regiment, but they had a disciplinary place in a town called Afir, about thirty kilometres from Dellys. It was right in the middle of nowhere, in bandit country, next to a big forest called la Mizrana, which was a rebel hideout. The forest of Mizrana had absolutely everything the rebels could wish for, including a whole hospital. We had a helicopter which would pick us up and take us to problem places. I spent the best part of two years in that section. All of us were conscripted men, apart from two of the officers, both of whom got killed in action. During the two years I spent in that company we lost our captain, our lieutenant, and quite a few of my friends: all killed. I was told that when you hear the bullet whizzing around your ears, it is no good to get low, you are too late. If you hear the bullet, it means you have not been touched by it. It was one of the officers who told us that. But I can't remember being frightened, it was more that I was alert to the danger. We used to go sometimes for as long as eight days, moving from village to village, sleeping rough at night,

15. Life in the army …

16. A different way of getting around …

in wait for the rebels who were hoping to come out from the forest, which sometimes they did. We would eat figs, dates, anything you could forage. Since that time I have never been able to bear dates. Disgusting! The most horrible thing you can eat.

I saw atrocities committed on both sides. I remember going into a village where the rebels had come in the night and slit the throat of a Muslim gentleman who was living there. His decorations and honours, including his military cross were pinned on the wall. And they cut his throat.

But I also remember seeing, on operations, people who had been condemned to death by the French: Muslims, so-called rebels, digging their own burial plots in the evenings. In the morning they were killed and buried in the graves they had dug. I saw a village where the French army had found a cave full of ammunition and supplies. They tied up the guy who they found there, put TNT on his leg and blew up the whole bloody lot, the house and the man. So there was no mercy on either side. It was all what I would call the atrocities of war. Though of course we were not considered to be at war. We were 'peacekeeping', sleeping with our guns by our sides.

At the end of the day, I did not know why we were there. I morally objected to what we were doing. I saw General de Gaulle visiting the camp, making speeches, telling us soldiers that Algeria was French, and I always remember when he said, 'From Algiers to Boulogne, there is only France.' We believed him. Little did we know that he was already negotiating to get out of the situation.

That's when the problems in France started. Several

generals rebelled. It was a sad moment in the history of France. Some of those generals – the leader was General Salan, the most decorated soldier in the army – had been instrumental in bringing de Gaulle back to power. The head of the Navy, the head of the Air Force, and Salan who had been Commander in Chief in Algeria – lined up against de Gaulle's idea of coming out of Algeria. But their rebellion failed. In its wake the government soldiers looked for Salan everywhere, but he escaped. He was condemned to death and then captured, but his sentence was changed to life imprisonment. The other generals received the same punishment.

There had been one general who hadn't participated in this coup, called Massu, a paratrooper. A few years later, in 1968, during the uprisings in France, de Gaulle had to go and ask the army whether it supported him or not, because he wasn't confident in their support. So he went to see Massu, who was in Germany at the time. Massu's answer was that he was willing to support him, but in return de Gaulle would have to pardon the generals. So they were no longer imprisoned, they were simply retired, the whole situation had all been cleaned up. But that was 1968: we were ready for a revolution which did not happen. De Gaulle called on the people to protest in the street, and more than a million people went onto the Champs Élysées to protest against what was happening and rally to his name. The communist party, which was still quite strong in France, abstained from rebelling against de Gaulle. So the rebellion collapsed. Things went back to semi-normal, and de Gaulle stayed in power.

I was anti-Gaullist; I felt we should not have left Algeria.

17. Far from home

But then I felt we should not have fought the war in Algeria at all, the conflict should have been avoided. I don't blame de Gaulle for getting us involved, I blame the politicians: they should have seen what was coming and accepted the fact that Algeria was not French. To start with, the majority of the population was Muslim. A large minority, of about two million roughly, were of European origin. There were many people of Spanish origin, and a large contingent from Alsace Lorraine, and they had been there for centuries. I would say that in the section where I was stationed, half of the local people had opted to stay French.

The tragedy is that we left behind thousands of *pieds noirs* – native Algerians who supported French rule – to be slaughtered, because they had no French passport. Many did flee; there was a huge influx of refugees and we tried to assimilate them, which is why about 11 per cent of the French population is Muslim. Some went to Corsica, and others to mountainous regions like Corrèzes, which had empty villages. But they were never properly welcomed by the French. We should not have lost Algeria like that. We should have negotiated long before it happened, to stay there in friendship and association. We should not have got involved in the tragedy that unfolded. The French government has only very recently given an official apology for the way the *pieds noirs* were treated. So it still does not feel resolved.

For myself, when what should have been the end of my tour came up, I wasn't allowed to leave, because the situation was so bad. I was taken back into the army for another six months. Finally though, my time came and I could go home.

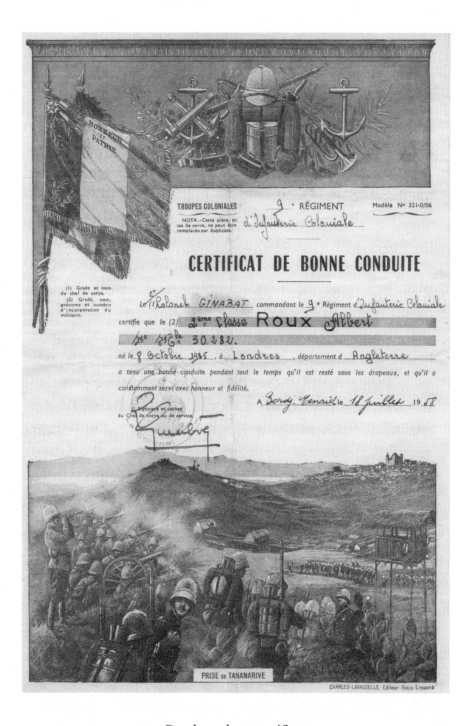

18. Good conduct certificate

Unfortunately, I had to leave my dog Sultanne there: she was an army dog and had to stay behind. That did cause me great pain at the time. But the day arrived, the transport appeared and brought me back to Algiers, and at last I was back on the boat that had brought me all that time before. Back to the mother country. I hadn't been to France, hadn't left Algeria, in all that time.

So there I was, heading home, first stop Marseilles. As soon as I disembarked, I kissed the ground; I was so happy to be back. I spent the night in Marseilles, and the next morning took a train to Paris. I got my Certificate of Good Conduct from the army, saying I had served with honour and fidelity during my years 'under the flag'. I'm not sure that that was true. But I was out. It was 1958, and I was twenty-three. It was a strange feeling, going back to civilian life. My time in Algeria did mark me, that's for sure. I had nightmares. And for a good part of a year afterwards, whenever I heard a bang, I used to duck. The experience had hardened me, and certainly I understood far more about life when I left the army than I did before I joined. I was more a man and no longer a boy.

# 5

## The Cazalets

Once I was out of the army, I had to start thinking about finding a job. For me, there wasn't any question: I was going back to Britain. I took the boat again, Calais to Dover. However, when I got to Customs in Dover the official was not happy with my paperwork. Not only did he deny me entry, but he stamped a red cross in my passport. I always remember what he wrote: 'Persona Non Grata'. He wanted to make sure I didn't come back. I had a girlfriend waiting to meet my train at Victoria station. Well, the train from Dover did arrive, but I was not on it. It was rather sad. I spent the night there in Dover, waiting for the next morning's boat, guarded by a bobby who taught me how to play crib, and showed me how the policemen smuggled duty-free cigarettes in under their helmets.

So instead of London, I found myself back with my mother in Paris. She was still living in the same flat in Saint Mandé.

Michel was living there too, doing his apprenticeship. I looked desperately for a job. First, I found employment as a dustman – I would have taken anything. So there I was, emptying dustbins. Well, they have to be emptied. I did that for a couple of weeks, but I still belonged to the Society of Bakery at Saint Michel, so once a week I would go there to find out if there were jobs available. Week after week there was nothing, until finally one day in the newspaper *France Soir* I spotted an ad for a job in the British embassy in Paris. The kitchen was looking for a washer-up. Hallelujah! I went for a quick interview, and was engaged as a potwash. What's more, the job was clearly marked as living-in, so the funny thing was that after being deported as a persona non grata I was suddenly back in England, because the embassy of course was English territory.

I used to do my duties as a potwash as quickly as possible so I could go back in the kitchen and see what was happening. After a couple of weeks of this, it piqued the interest of the chef, Emil Rouault, who invited me into his office and asked if I was interested in cooking. I said, 'Well, actually that is my job.' I explained that I had served a three-year apprenticeship in pastry, and I had a couple of years cheffing in the UK. He asked me how I had ended up as a washer-up and once I had explained he said, 'That's fine, I'll take you on in the kitchen.' So I transferred from being potwash to working in the kitchen, and eventually became his number two.

In this capacity, I got to know the ambassador, Sir Gladwyn Jebb, and his wife, and their daughter, who was a great friend of Princess Margaret – the princess came and visited the embassy on several occasions. The Jebbs were intrigued by the little Frenchman in the washing-up area who could speak good English. Much of the work we did was cooking on a grand scale, not only for the embassy itself, but also because we used sometimes to go to the Élysées Palace when they were very busy with banquets for de Gaulle. After I had been there some time my brother Michel finished his apprenticeship and was looking for work. I suggested he apply for the position of pastry chef and he was taken on there. So for the first time, for a short while, we were working in the same kitchen.

It was at this time that Monique, my first wife, came into my life properly. Actually, I had known her for some time, but I had not thought of her in that way. She had gone to the local school in St Mandé, in the same class as my brother — she was the same age as he was — and she used to live on the sixth floor of our building, while we were on the first floor. So she sometimes came to our flat and spent time with my mother. That was where I first met her, briefly, before I went to Algeria. As far as she was concerned it was love at first sight and she fell deeply in love with me at the tender age of fourteen years old; but then I went away. We only really met for two days or so then.

By the time I got back to Paris she had moved out of that flat and was living elsewhere in a little apartment because she had been having a bit of a dispute with her mother. But one day I was walking out of my mother's flat and I looked up and there she was, peering out of her mother's window because she had come to visit for the day. And so we met again. I started to take her out: she had obviously grown up and was

now a young lady. She was a sales girl in a boutique on the
Faubourg St Honoré, not far from the British embassy, selling
lingerie. From that time on our relationship became serious.
We would meet nearly every day after we had both finished
work. We would go for walks and to restaurants, or back to
the little one-bedroomed flat she had. Although she lived on
her own, her grandmother was looking after her, so once a
week we would go for dinner there. She used to be very firm
with me about Monique: 'You have to look after her. And don't
do anything you shouldn't.' Though actually we did whatever
we wanted.

After about a year at the embassy – a very happy year – I
started looking for a job elsewhere because, though I enjoyed
it, the embassy job was not that well paid. The ambassadress
knew that I wanted to move on: I had told her that one day
I wanted to go back to England, come what may. She helped
guide me through the process, and offers of employment
began to come in: one from Emperor Haile Selassie to work
as his chef in Addis Ababa, one from the Duchess of Alba,
and one from the British ambassador in Washington DC.
I told him I would think about it. And then one day after
lunch I was asked to go see the ambassadress who wanted
to introduce me to one of her guests who was staying for a
couple of days. That was Mrs Cazalet. For me, it was love at
first sight with that lady. The way she talked, her elegance,
her charm: I was enthralled with everything about her, and I
dearly wanted to go and work for her. She explained to me they
were looking for a chef, and I told her that if she kindly put
an offer in then I would consider it. Once she had made me an

offer on paper, my decision was taken – the Cazalets it would be. It was that introduction that led not only to eight happy years of my life at their house, Fairlawne, but eventually to Le Gavroche itself.

Mrs Cazalet applied for the permit, which duly gave me a five-year stay in England. I got my little green book, with which I would have to report to the Alien's Office on a yearly basis. The whole thing happened very fast. I said to Monique: 'I have been offered the job in England, but it's got to be now, so we haven't got much time to be married.' Her answer was immediate: 'We'll find the time.' And we did manage to get married – not in a church at that point, but in a civil ceremony. It was a small affair – just our families, even Monique's mother, although they were still not getting on that well at the time. She had to be there to sign the papers because Monique was only eighteen, and in France at the time you didn't legally come of age until you were twenty-one. We had lunch with both our families together, and that was it; we didn't have enough money to make a big fuss. Monique was happy to come to England with me, even though she was leaving everything she knew in Paris. She would have gone anywhere – she was devoted. Because she spoke not a word of English, I thought it was safest to go to the Cazalets for a couple of months to settle in and see that the job was the right one. And so I set off: I was on my way.

~

What a beautiful house Fairlawne was; what a wonderful place. An elegant house, red brick and white stone, with wings and pediments like a miniature castle, set in the green fields and parkland of the Kent countryside. It was an absolutely stunning estate. There were massive expanses of lawn, greenhouses, and huge ponds full of trout. Major Peter Cazalet, my new boss, was a famous racehorse trainer who trained the Queen Mother's horses – one of the most celebrated of these was Devon Loch, who had fallen in the last furlong of the Grand National under Dick Francis – so to my delight I found myself back among horses.

The Cazalet family were absolutely fantastic from the very beginning. For a start, I never felt like a servant there – I was part of a team. They entertained in style. Mrs Cazalet could have been in charge of a five- or six-star hotel, and she would have run it with precision and perfection. To her, etiquette and manners were second nature, and they extended those manners to the staff as much as they did to their guests. She would never enter the kitchen, for instance, without ringing and asking if it was convenient to come with a guest. The Queen Mother would come to stay at Fairlawne quite often, and Lady Cazalet would ring down and say, 'The Queen Mother is leaving and would like to say thank you. Is it convenient to come?' And she would always knock at the door, which would surprise me – it was her kitchen in her own house!

I can't find the words to describe that lady, and the family in general. There were two sons, Victor and Anthony, who were still quite young, so I had to feed the nursery and nanny as well. Sir Peter had two older children also – grown up by the time I arrived. They were from his first marriage, to P.G. Wodehouse's daughter, who had very sadly died: Edward Cazalet, who became a high court judge, and Sheran, who married the chairman of WHSmith.

And so I plunged into this new life: this was the first time I had been in charge of my own kitchen, yet it felt totally natural. My first job was to find out what the family liked and disliked. The best chef in the world is the one who most pleases his boss. Take mushrooms, for example: Major Cazalet did not like the little button mushrooms, he liked the big old-fashioned black ones. So at breakfast I always made sure he had his old mushrooms, secreting black juice. They didn't seem very appetising to me, but that's what he liked. He liked his grouse also: it was the custom that people would send birds that they shot to their friends, so I would receive the grouse which had been sent to him, and pluck and prepare them. I remember one evening cooking a brace of them for him. He had one and a half, and when the other half came back what did Chef do with it? Well, he ate it, because it's one of my favourite birds. The next morning I prepared the boss's breakfast as usual for nine o'clock – he used to go riding at five thirty in the morning and come back at nine for breakfast, so I always did a large breakfast of scrambled eggs and kippers and all the things that he liked. That morning he called me and said, 'Chef, could I have that half of grouse I left last night . . .'

*Oh shit*, I thought, and I said to him, 'I'm very, very sorry, sir – I ate it.' There was a pause, and then I said, 'My God, it was nice.'

And he smiled. 'That's OK, Chef,' he said, 'as long as you enjoyed it.'

As for Mrs Cazalet: she was wonderful, divine in talent and knowledge, a real society lady. The family often had house parties of guests over the weekends, and to take the orders to plan for this was always a joy. On the Wednesday or Thursday morning beforehand I would take up my notebook and go to see her. She would be there cutting the flowers, talking to the gardeners about what she needed for each room: she did all the arrangements of all the flowers in every room herself. So she would be asking the gardeners, 'Could I have this, could I have that?' I would join her with my book and we would talk about the menu, the people who were coming. Everything was meticulously planned in advance, the right menus for each particular guest. She had everything in her logbook: the name of the guest, what they had eaten last time, what they liked and disliked. She was highly methodical. At the same time she would be talking to the kids – they would come rushing down and she would stop them in their stride and say, 'Have you said hello to Chef?' The kids would come back and say, 'Hello, Chef,' and off they'd go. I would have gone to the fire for her; she was an extraordinary woman.

The Cazalets had provided me with a lovely cottage in the village of Shipbourne and Mrs Cazalet had it all refurbished and painted the outside pink. It was known as the Pink Cottage. It was my first ever house; before that I had been living in, at the embassy and in all my other jobs. I was used to small rooms or our tiny flat or the barracks in Algeria, so this felt very new. I remember writing to Monique after a couple of weeks and saying, 'Prepare to come; I have found paradise.' Which I really had. This was a proper house for us, with three bedrooms, a very large dining room, a tiny little kitchen, and a big garden where I could do all the gardening. I loved that; I had my vegetables and I kept rabbits and fed the pigeons. Our neighbours were charming people – we quickly made friends with several couples and our families would spend time together. We acquired a little Labrador, called Sultanne in memory of the dog I had left in Algeria and of the original Sultanne of my childhood. Eventually, after we had opened our restaurant, the new Sultanne had babies, and we kept one and named her Gavroche – the urchin. The name suited her – she was a very mischievous dog. Always eating what she shouldn't. From that time in Shipbourne onwards I have never been without a dog, sometimes having four of them. Dogs are amazing creatures. Now that I am older and I have a little difficulty walking, my current dog, Canelou, a beautiful chestnut Labrador, is so cautious with me. Every time I walk in she looks carefully at me before coming in front of me slowly, to check she is not tripping me. To me, dogs bring humans a warmth which is very often needed.

The kitchen at Fairlawne was all set up when I arrived – a good, decent kitchen, with a pantry and a scullery. There was a huge stove – far larger than an Aga – that worked day and night. Once again there was an old man whose main job it was to look after the stove, clean it, and remove the ashes. The house was run just like *Upstairs Downstairs*. There was a butler, Mr Bradbrooke, two footmen, a lady's maid, a nanny for the children, the chauffeur, a scullery boy, and gardeners – lots of gardeners. Monique became my helper in the kitchen.

I was the apple of Mrs Cazalet's eye, I knew that. There was a rapport between us: anything I asked for, she would always make sure that I got it. When I arrived I asked for good copper pans to be bought, and they were, and not long after we also installed some freezers. I used to work very closely with the gardeners. The house had a proper, lovely kitchen garden: red-brick wall, cold frame, greenhouses. They grew everything: peaches and grapes in the greenhouse, all the vegetables you needed in the garden. It was state of the art. There was always something to be dug up and something to plant, and in my spare time I would help turn the earth and put manure down and compost. Tending the earth, both there and in my own garden at the Pink Cottage, was one of my favourite things to do. And when I went to France I used to bring back some seeds and give them to the gardener, and teach them for instance that in France French beans were not hugely long and skinny, they were little and more delicate. The boss loved those beans, I remember that. Or I would bring the gardeners seeds for little chantenay carrots as opposed to great big coarse ones. At that time in Britain the quality of the vegetables wasn't typically judged by the taste, it was judged by the size – enormous giant marrows and leeks which were not very good to eat. But I had access to wonderful ingredients at Fairlawne: as well as the racing stables the Cazalets had a farm there. They even had an abattoir: the best bits would come to us, and the rest would go to the local butcher. So the journey from the field to the table was short.

I always felt I was a part of that huge family. I had a job to do. And Mrs Cazalet used to say to me quite often, 'We like you, Chef, not only for your cooking but for your discretion.' I knew what she meant, because that was the sort of life that they had. They were pampered, yes; there were butlers, a lady's maid, chefs, what have you. But it was not a life that I would have liked. There was no real privacy: there was always a servant somewhere. Everything you did was observed. Not by me, though; I was there for a purpose which was clearly defined. That purpose was to feed the family happily and cook what they liked, and I have to say I succeeded. But there was always chit-chat among the other staff. Servants, I have discovered, like to talk. Private service in those days was all, 'Did you know what she did? Did you hear what he said . . . ?' And so on and so on. They listened at the door and peered through the peephole, but they didn't talk to me about it because right at the beginning I said to them: 'Not me. I am the chef. I am there to cook their dinner. And I'm in love with them. So what they do, it is their problem. They don't encroach on my privacy and I don't intend to encroach on theirs.' The family knew that that was my attitude. I did my job to the best of my ability; I cooked, and then I took my bike and went off to my little cottage, and that was it. So there was a sort of a bond between me and the family, and it still exists, with the children, who I see to this day.

My love for horses, which had started in my childhood and at Gamlingay, started to grow even further while I was at

Fairlawne. So much so that I used to ride with the string some mornings. Major Cazalet was rather proud to have a chef who was so interested in the stables. I would go out with the first string every morning, then come back to the house before they started off with the second string to cook breakfast for him and his guests. On my day off on Mondays, I would go and see him in the morning when I knew he was going to the races, to Lingfield or wherever, and say, 'If there is a little space in the car, I would love to go.' And he invariably would say, 'Of course, Chef, you can certainly ride with me in the car.' So I would go to the races, chauffeur driven; I'd get out of the car, with my badge and everything, and off I would go. His last words would always be, 'Don't gamble too much.'

Monique became pregnant quite soon after we arrived, and in 1960, after we had been at Fairlawne for a year and a bit, my son Michel was born, at Tonbridge Wells. Ambury hospital was the sort of hospital that they had during the war, made of wood – it was a kind of barracks, really. I cannot explain the joy that it gave me when I learned I was the father of a son. I was really over the moon.

When Michel was born we wanted to have a christening, and for that we had to get married in a church, because so far we had only had the civil ceremony in France. So we had a church wedding in Tonbridge at the same time as Michel's christening. Again, it was very small, just the family who came from France and that was it. It was a very happy day. My first wife can only be described as an angel; she was a very giving mother, extremely devoted to the children and to me. I had a very happy marriage, lasting thirty years. How

19.  Monique and Michel Jr – a celebration

did she manage to put up with all my dilly-dally? Only deep deep love can do that. Because in that way, I was not always a good husband. I have always had a weakness when it comes to women.

When Michel was a toddler, my wife and I used to take him with us to the kitchens. We would put him under the huge kitchen table with a bit of pastry and a small roller, and he would make his own 'cake'. When he was quite happy with it he would emerge from under the table and give it to me to put in the Aga to cook. He has always been an exceptional kid.

One day when he was very young he crawled out of the kitchen without us realising it. He went through the door in the corner that led to the main part of the house. It had a long red carpet – and he went crawling off down it. Somehow he got into the main house, and it happened to be a weekend when the Queen Mum was visiting. So of course, it was she who found him. The first thing I knew about it was when she appeared in the kitchen with Michel in her arms. 'Chef, I think this is yours?' she said, handing him back.

The Queen Mother came to stay quite often, as did other members of the royal family. There were usually distinguished people there at weekends. Elizabeth Taylor came many times – she was a good friend of the Cazalet's daughter Sheran. Christopher Soames, who would go on to become a friend and great patron of the Gavroche, was there a lot. Then there was Douglas Fairbanks Jr and his wife. Obviously the whole racing world came there – ever since then, every time I go to Cheltenham or Epsom or Newmarket, a famous jockey or the son of a famous jockey will pop in and say hello, because at some point in the past I have fed them all. The weekends would be about cooking grand beautiful food, while the weekdays were simpler, just the family.

Three years after we arrived, in 1963, I had a car crash. I was coming home one Saturday morning after doing the breakfast. The Cazalets were going racing, so I didn't have to do a formal lunch – I had prepared some for the staff and gone home, and there was a car in front of me going very slowly because the people in it were canoodling. And when I tried to overtake and saw there was another car coming, there wasn't enough time, so we ended up meeting in the ditch. I had waited for my new car with the registration number 13, and I got it. Was it a good 13 or a bad 13, we'll never know: because although I had a crash that was bad, perhaps I could have been dead instead. As it was I was in hospital for three months with my hip in traction. But again the Cazalets were very understanding – Monique took over my role in the kitchen for a while. She would come and visit me with Michel every day, and we had a very kind neighbour who came and fetched her afterwards. I recovered well in the end, but it was a difficult time.

A few years after Michel was born, I had a daughter, Danielle. A little bit of a rebel, as sometimes girls can be, but totally lovable, and I seem to recall she had me running along her finger. I'm still extremely close to both my children. I've never had a bad word with my son. Michel chose to follow my profession of his own free will. Like me, he started with an apprenticeship in pâtisserie, and he chose to do this in France. I remember the day before he left, he came back from

20. With my mother at Fairlawne

shopping with a huge Union Jack. I said, 'What is that? Why are you taking that to France?' He said, 'Dad, that is going to be my bedcover.' He is very British, to the point that he fully understands cricket, which is more than I can claim. Danielle is the same. Although now she lives in Nice where she is an English teacher in a private school, if you asked her her nationality she would straightaway say, 'I'm English.'

My mother came to see us in the UK quite often, and at around this time Mrs Cazalet told me that she was in need of a lady's maid. I mentioned my mother, and she got the job: a permit was applied for and so my mother spent a couple of years at Shipbourne with us. It worked very well. My mother and Mrs Cazalet got along famously, and I was happy to give her the opportunity to be in such a wonderful place. She was a real help with the children. They loved their time with her – she would take them on walks and go picking wild strawberries and chestnuts and watercress.

My brother Michel was working as a private chef for the Rothschilds in France, so we didn't get to see a huge amount of each other, but he would come over too, and sometimes he would cook in the Fairlawne kitchens with me. I remember him making his magnificent sugar works there, because he was starting in his competition work as a pastry chef. He would spend his time working on the blown sugar – not just things like roses, but huge creations, whole pineapples, animals, scenes, which would win prizes. We would talk in those days about the dream we had of opening a restaurant.

Whenever anyone from the family came – my sisters often stayed with us too – they would bring food parcels with

21. On the terrace at Fairlawne, with family
including Michel (far right)

them. There would be fine cheeses, because you couldn't get good cheese like Camembert in England, and garlic sausage, saucissons, dried hams. All of it was impossible to get in England at the time; even olive oil was not considered something to cook with here. It was for putting in your ears. So it would be a real treat to sit down as a family and devour these goodies.

Certainly my children had a very different childhood to my own. We decided they should have an English education. There was never any question of them going to the Lycée Français. By the time they were born, my love of Great Britain was even stronger than when I first set foot in the country, so there was no question: the kids were going to be British and they were going to have a British education. When they were little they went to a school in the village, and in the afternoon they spent time with their grandmother, running around the fields – it was a lovely childhood.

Then, the bombshell hit. When Michel was six and Danielle was four all our lives changed. It must have been a great shock to them: we were off to Tooting, London, to live in a semi-detached house in a great big city. My years in Fairlawne were some of the happiest of my life, but I was about to embark on something new, the realisation of a dream. And once again, I had the Cazalets to thank for it.

The whole Cazalet family knew of my desire to one day open a restaurant, and one early morning after breakfast the boss called me into his study for a chit-chat. His private secretary was there, so I knew it was to be a serious talk. What he said to me was to change my life: 'Chef, we know in the family that you want to open your own restaurant and we are all behind it. We can help you with it, but I'd like you to spend another two years with us, and then after that I will write you a cheque for £500. As a gift.' I just couldn't believe it. A gift! Back in 1967, £500 was about a third of the total investment of the restaurant, and he was giving it to me with no strings attached. He said, 'Furthermore we will invest that £500 in shares now, and we are usually quite good on picking up shares, as you must know, Chef.' (This was a joke because he knew the butler and I used to share the investing tips we gleaned from him.) That £500 went into a company called Elliot Automation – a large public company which was in charge of all the traffic lights in the UK. It was bought out by Arnold Weinstock of GEC, who was to become a dear friend. Many years later, he invested in one of my businesses, and he used to tease me about its progress, asking me, 'When am I going to get dividends?' And I used to say, 'Well Arnold, what about Elliot Automation? I lost money on that.' Because the £500, by the time of my departure from the Cazalets, had become £250. But the old man, true to his word, gave me the full £500. He was an honourable man.

Finally, in that meeting, Major Cazalet said, 'I will ask some of my friends to form a syndicate to participate also.' Which he did; true to his word, he talked to some of his friends, and six of them chipped in as well. It was quite an illustrious group of people: his sister invested, and Edward, his oldest son. And some other friends as well. This yielded another £500, for which I gave away 30 per cent of the company. But not to the old man. He took nothing in return: it was purely a gift. One of the investors was Michael von Clemm. He was an amazing man – six foot tall and brilliant, with a doctorate from Harvard. He was a fascinating individual who would go on to become head of Credit Suisse bank and help invent the concept of the Canary Wharf development. Eventually he would become chairman of Le Gavroche and a lifelong friend.

We did ask the Rothschild family, who my brother Michel had been working for five years, if they wanted to participate – they refused. The sister of Baron Guy de Rothschild sent a letter to Mrs Cazalet – they were friends – saying they would not invest as they had never really liked my brother. But we had enough from the other investors and from the Cazalets.

What happened after that is history.

# 6

## Our Vision

When I first came to this country, I could see there was a gap in the market. In Paris, the restaurant world was blooming; there were lots of restaurants, big brasseries were open and thriving. In London, everything was different: there were no real ingredients, and the food being served was not great quality. Even at that stage I felt it would be nice to have a restaurant with my brother. I always thought that there was a vacuum, as far as restaurants were concerned; it felt like the country was ready for a revolution to happen.

It was to be many years before we realised this dream. Before we started, I went all around all those 'French' restaurants in London: Mirabelle, L'Ecu de France, Quaglinos, and tasted some of their wares. I wanted to study what was on offer here; I wanted to find out what the opposition was made of. They all had the same model: big menus, lots of dishes, heavy food. I have a collection of menus from around the world, and when I look at the ones from those restaurants I wonder how they managed. Mind you, they would have had sixty, eighty, even a hundred cooks in the kitchen to handle that. There were five or six top restaurants, so called, serving the food of the moment, and there were some fantastic dishes amongst it all. But there was no alternative to those restaurants, so there was the same crowd, going from one to another night after night. There were these principal restaurants, and then hotels like the Connaught or the Savoy, and the gentlemen's clubs. The clubs mostly served grey and brown food – devilled kidneys on toast, steak and kidney pudding. Then there might be some Indian and Italian places, but all low quality. And then at the other end of the scale there were the Lyons Corner Houses. There was a big gap apart from that.

I had been to the Parisian restaurants also. I saved to go to experiment, to see what was out there. I went to the Tour d'Argent, which still is in my view one of the best restaurants in the world, not specifically for the food, but for the surroundings; it's an extremely romantic spot, overlooking Notre Dame. It's lovely. I have my own table there, even today, though I haven't been for a while. The service there was fantastic. You sneezed, and a handkerchief would appear: it was like being in a musical. Maxim's, on the other hand, I found very disappointing. I had wanted to go there since I was a child, and for my first encounter I took my wife. It was clearly a prestigious establishment, you could tell from the moment you arrived. Then the waiter came: he was a chichi waiter, a snooty waiter, and he became shirty with us. When I asked a question about the menu, he drew himself up, craned his neck, and said, 'M'sieur. M'sieur, of course, *of course* it is hot' – because, silly boy that I was, I had asked whether a dish was served hot or cold. And then, as he made to take the order, he put his pad on the table. I got up, then, and said, 'Perhaps you want to be seated? You know what, young man, why don't you pull a chair up and be comfortable?' At this you could see he was shaken: he went red round the face. He suddenly realised he was dealing with someone who knew a bit about how things should be done, and he apologised. After that it was all very different, the tone changed and he was very respectful. But I was disappointed with the food and the service: I never returned.

On the other hand, I went back to Mirabelle many times, mostly to have the brioche with marrow and sauce bordelaise. It's a wonderful dish: you have the brioche, and inside that there is poached marrow and bordelaise sauce. To my palate, that was the ultimate: delicious, old-fashioned cuisine. The service there was like an opera: it was all Italian, all singing different songs. It was a bit of a cacophony, hearing about the dog of the neighbour, typical Italian service. Which is terrific, because when an Italian is good in service he is much better than the Frenchman. They are born to serve, and they have that knack, that graciousness that makes you happy. The English? They can be shirty – but they are also better than the French. The French are arrogant. Things have improved a lot in England. There is still is a lot to be done, but while standards are improving here, in France they are dropping.

Countless meetings took place between Michel and myself to formulate the idea of our restaurant. To expose it, refine it, so that we could bring it to life. The aim was to give our customers pleasure: to promote a relaxed atmosphere where joy could flourish. The old-fashioned restaurant model was what we wanted to transform. We wanted something different. I had a vision – anybody who starts a new business has to have a vision – that my restaurant would not feel like a restaurant. It would feel like a private establishment, one that the customers were invited to as guests. That feeling would start at the door – as soon as the customers came in, there would be a warmth. It was the job of the front of house to ensure that. Then, the menu would be streamlined so the customers would know that what they were getting was prepared with perfect technique and tip-top ingredients. We wanted to be true and faithful to French gastronomy, and that starts at the beginning, with the best possible ingredients. All the details would be perfect, so we would use classic French recipes and techniques. What would set us apart was the quality, of the technique and of the ingredients. So for instance, take a lobster with garlic butter: you could get this in other establishments, but the difference with us would be in the way it was cooked, and the fact that it was perfectly fresh lobster. Or smoked trout with green sauce – the green sauce would be made the real way, with chlorophyll and herbs, home made, and with the mayonnaise done properly and served at the right temperature. And I would have searched out that trout myself to find the best one.

For this it was essential to have a small, seasonal menu, and that was what it became. The reason that it should be short was that that allowed us to use the best possible ingredients, celebrate them, and use them when they were absolutely fresh. There was no division between Michel and myself on that score – there was plenty of division about the business and how it should direct itself, but not on the size and the frame of the menu. It was a consensus of both brothers, a distillation of what we both felt. There was a lot of discussion on it. We would have no more than six or seven dishes each for the starters, five meat, three fish, five desserts. That was the à la carte menu, and on top of that we had a small *Le Chef Propose* menu, the size of a notelet, on which we would have a couple of dishes each, inspired usually by the ingredients I had picked up in the market that day.

I've always succumbed to the pressure of adapting my sort of cooking to English taste. In those days there was quite a different culture of food in England, so when people used to observe – not complain exactly, but observe – that there was no sugar in the salads, I would say, 'No, I don't put it in myself, but if you want me to put sugar in yours, I will do so.' You used to give some people the food you had cooked, and the first thing they would do was grab the salt grinder and flood it with salt. Then they would say, 'Excuse me, this dish is too salty!' And I would say, 'Yes it is. You did your own cooking. You did not even taste it.'

'Well,' they would say, 'I'm very sorry, but I can't eat it. Can you do me another one?'

That was England at the time. That has changed.

I remember the very first menu: Watercress soup – *Crème*

*de Cresson*, 6 shillings and sixpence. *Soufflé Suissesse*, a dish for two – 19 shillings. *Omelette Rothschild* for two – 30 shillings. There were rillettes and pâtés for starters. The best of shellfish – lobster and langoustine, sole and turbot. For main courses we had not just wonderful grilled steak and chicken with Armagnac sauce, but the famous *Caneton Gavroche* – a whole duck poached in consommé with three sauces. And as a real speciality, for four persons you could order the *Selle de Veau Orloff.* These were all dishes that used classic French technique.

You had to study commodities and to be very careful when you calculate the price, so as not to overprice things. That way, you can put yourself out of business. Because at the end of the day you need to make money, money being an essential in life. Obviously you have to love your speciality, so to speak, because as soon as you like something you put all your energy and heart into it. And then of course the end result is much better. But quite a lot of those businesses go bust because they overreach themselves: people can't afford it any more. We never had that. I attribute my success with this to being observant, and defining what is the market of tomorrow, let alone today. What we were doing was creating what people wanted, it was just that they did not yet know what that was.

For the business side, I read extensively: how to form a company, how to run it, how to keep minutes, hold board meetings and all the rest. You can teach yourself these things, I always believe that. So I made sure the Gavroche was run according to the book on all levels. We were scrupulous about having board meetings every month, and AGMs every year.

Everything was minuted and acted on. I am fascinated by the business side, and an avid reader of management books and the *Financial Times*. If you want to run a business, it needs to be done properly.

I wanted the restaurant to be a destination, so it didn't need to open in Piccadilly. It needed to be in a quiet corner of London, somewhere where people could park. My brother's idea was not quite the same. He would have loved a country house with a few rabbits and chickens. Something which had a feeling of love – we both felt that. We did come close to a place that matched his ideal – we found somewhere in Guildford where Michel could have had his chickens, and pigs, and a bit of greenery. But we would not have had the society clientele. We went to go and have a look at it, and came close to going with it. But I had also been to a firm called Ackroyd and Sons, a broker whose speciality was selling restaurants, and they came up with a place in Lower Sloane Street. It had been an Italian restaurant, called Canova, next door to a hairdresser. It was exactly what I felt Le Gavroche should be: away from the crowd, ample parking out front. It had a lovely ceramic floor. As a restaurant, it was awful; I love Italian food, but this was not even really Italian. Michel came and had a look at it. It was not in the country, to his great sorrow. Where would the chickens go, and the little pig? That was part of his dream. But we decided that this, finally, was the place. We made an offer to buy which was duly accepted.

Although the restaurant was terrible, the general manager was Italian, and he was wonderful: his name was Antonio Batistella, and he would come to play a big part in our lives.

I dined there a couple of times with the family – incognito – and I liked what I saw of Antonio. Once we had bought the place I asked him to stay on and he became a saviour.

For the first couple of months, before we could put our plan into action, we kept the restaurant as it was, but changed the menu to a French one. I did the cooking with some help from my wife, and we kept it ticking over and got some new customers who enjoyed our food. After two months, we closed, and ripped out all the interiors ready for our transformation. Everything was gone – kitchens, fridges, furniture, tables – all stripped out overnight to prepare for our new vision. I said to Antonio and the other two members of staff who were working at Canova, 'Look, it's going to take three months before we open. I'll pay you. Just go on holiday, I'll want you back.' They took the money. One of them went on holiday and didn't come back. Antonio and the other one returned, and stayed for years. Antonio was wonderful: very committed, very honest. He was a person I could trust completely, a good Christian, and above all, he became a very dear friend. The other stayed with us for several years and became the wine sommelier.

Because we had never had a restaurant before, everything had to be learnt from scratch: how to hire staff, how to direct staff, how to prepare the weekly wages and so forth. Perhaps one of the biggest changes from our lives before was going from being pretty much in sole charge of the kitchen to having a team, because there is a big difference between having only yourself to organise and opening up a restaurant with a team of five or six in the kitchen. In a restaurant you have to give orders and expect the job to be done to the right standard. It is a different skill. Then the company had to be formed, and run. Minutes had to be taken. The kitchen had to be designed and equipped, and so did the restaurant itself. Through connections of the Cazalets we appointed David Mlinaric, a designer who was already a well-known figure. He had a very illustrious father-in-law who had won the Victoria Cross in Greece during the German invasion. I gave David a free hand; I have never believed that you appoint someone and tell them their job. My opinion is, let them do what they are expert in, or otherwise don't appoint them and save money. He became very interested in the project – although he had done all sorts of other things beforehand, this was his first time designing a restaurant. We became long-time friends. He was very avant-garde, and this was reflected in his designs for the restaurant. He came up with a scheme which was sort of brownish, reddish – when I first saw the ideas mocked up, the colours looked awful to me: I had a job to understand how it would turn out. And then, through the connections of his wife Martha, and the connections of Edward Cazalet's wife, who had an art gallery, we landed a lot of Chagall prints. The décor when it clicked together was magic. It was acclaimed to be great news. There was the beautifully tiled mosaic floor, there were lots of banquettes and it was all a deep golden orange colour. Ochre, you could call it. It was equally rich and cosy: with its banquettes, and very plush curtains, it looked really opulent.

And so, Le Gavroche was born. The urchin.

# 7

---

# Beginnings

Finally the famous opening night arrived, on Saturday, 27 April 1967. There had been a bit of a problem beforehand because of the licences. Somehow our lawyers had forgotten to apply for a licence for that day. In those days there was always somebody objecting when you applied for an alcohol licence – either the neighbours or a local church would get annoyed. At the last minute we managed to get a special licence for twenty-four hours to get us through the opening. There was also a problem with the tables – we had carefully measured up for the correct size of table so they would allow for the greatest number of covers, but when the furniture arrived on the day of the opening, they were too big. Fortunately we did not need them for opening night, which was to be canapés and drinks, so we sent them immediately to be trimmed and had to hope they would be ready by Monday for the first night of diners.

Our preparations continued right up to the last minute, and then at exactly seven, people started to arrive. Mrs Cazalet, that divine person, had offered to send the invitations to our guests, and they all went out on her behalf. As she had put it when we discussed the opening: 'It would be nice if it was me presenting you.' And indeed it was. On the evening she was at the door, welcoming all her friends. I stood next to her, as they came in. 'Chef,' she would say, 'You remember the Duchess?' I find it hard to describe how touching that was for me – an acknowledgement of all the years I had worked for her. We invited about 150 people and to my astonishment about 150 people turned up, in a restaurant with a seating capacity of 100. It was packed. Anybody who had a name in London was there that evening. Ministers, artists, producers, you name it. Charlie Chaplin came, Robert Redford, Ava Gardner. Douglas Fairbanks and his wife, who had often stayed at Fairlawne. Anybody who wasn't there was seething with jealousy. It was pandemonium, real pandemonium. Everybody very smart and dressed up to the nines, with the ladies turning up in expensive coats – minks and furs. We soon ran out of tickets for coats, so that by the end we didn't even bother with a proper cloakroom system – we just put them in a pile. I remember towards the end of the evening the Duchess of Alba was desperately looking for a mink coat that had disappeared in the tumult. It was found, I'm glad to say.

I was upstairs on the restaurant floor that night. My brother was downstairs in the kitchen, in the basement. We served champagne and canapés – things like foie gras, French ingredients that you could not get in London. I remember vividly that great gourmet Christopher Soames, on the staircase leading to the kitchen, eating a cake of sorts, and observing that the peaches were not fresh peaches. That was very much in his style, but he was eating it, and it was good.

By midnight, the opening night was all finished and done. By the next morning, the restaurant was cleaned up and we were ready to open the doors for the first proper service. So the first real evening of trading arrived, and like magic, the restaurant was full; every table was booked. That was when we started to rack up cash, which was badly needed by that point. But what an amazing feeling, when suddenly, wham, you could feel the place taking off.

My first proper customers were the Cazalets – Mrs Cazalet, Sir Peter Cazalet and the two children. They had their dinner, and off they went. They offered to pay, I said, 'Absolutely not!' We wouldn't let them pay, because it's an old custom in my country of birth – when you open a restaurant the first customer doesn't pay. And besides, I am indebted to that family as long as I live.

It's true to say the restaurant has been full ever since. The press got hold of it, and there was never a table free. It was – success, just like that. After all that old guard of restaurants, suddenly there was this big explosion, this big change in how you could eat in London. The Roux brothers had arrived!.

As the weeks went on the numbers went on going up. We had a booking system so it was no good to come to the door to try and get a table, there were never any free. It was booked full from weeks, months in advance. The place was packed and the phone never stopped ringing. People came from all over the place – London, the countryside, further afield. Once we were featured in a magazine in the United States, the Americans started searching us out too.

All of this made us very busy in the kitchen. The kitchen wasn't large, to say the least. It was incredibly hot in there – no good for making pastry – because it was a basement with a central gas stove, and in those days ventilation systems were not great. There was an emergency hatch – with pull-down ladders like attics have – that went out onto the pavement. Occasionally we would open up the hatch a chink, just to let a bit of air in. Apart from that the only other opening was the stairs to the kitchen, and they acted like a chimney pulling all the smells up, so the first thing that hit you when you came in the back door was the smell of whatever was cooking. It reminded me of my childhood in Charolles – you could tell what was cooking by the waft you got as you came in. Sometimes we would have food chilling there on the steps because there was a draught going up there, and no other area to chill food down.

There were two dumb waiters that took the food from the kitchen to the restaurant floor, one for hot food and one for cold. Oh, I hated them. One or the other of them was always breaking down: at least once a month there would be waiters running up and down the stairs. Either that, or the waiters would be so busy they would leave the dumb waiter doors open at the top. That was a disaster, because of course the lift would not come back down. So then I would have an altercation with the front of house over the intercom about why the food wasn't being picked up. Since the intercom was on a false door at the back of the restaurant, sometimes the customers would be a bit surprised to hear us shouting at each other in French.

At the beginning, I couldn't let Michel loose in the dining room because he couldn't speak English very well. But slowly does it, he gradually eased in to the front of house. We would alternate in the kitchens: one week downstairs, one week upstairs. But Michel was never very good at recognising faces and people. One evening when he was on the floor, the restaurant was packed, and who should appear at the door but Princess Margaret. He approached her: 'Good evening, madame. Have you booked?'

'No,' she said, 'but you will find that my cousin the Earl of Litchfield has booked a table for six.' Of course Michel didn't know who the Earl of Litchfield was – he was simply one more customer to Michel. So he came rushing downstairs, and said, 'There is a woman upstairs who says she is the cousin of the Earl of Litchfield.'

So I went up to look. 'Well,' I said, 'that's Princess Margaret.'

'Ahhh,' said Michel. The maître d' came to the rescue and took her to her table.

It was the same with Stirling Moss. One night he came to the door. Now you have to remember that at that time everybody in the world knew the face of Stirling Moss; he was one of the most famous people in the country. Michel was at the door, and said, 'Can I have your name please, and have you booked?'

'Well yes,' he said, 'I'm Stirling Moss.'

'Ah, yah, got it,' said Michel. He came downstairs and said 'We've a guy upstairs called Stirling Moss. Is he famous?'

I said, 'Well, yeah, he's the greatest racing driver in the world.'

'Ahhh . . .' That was just like Michel.

Sometimes he got it the other way around. On the menu he had a dessert which he loved to make called *La Rose du Chef.* An example of his brilliant sugar work, this was a little sponge, covered in whipped cream flavoured with Grand Marnier, on top of which he used to put a rose made of sugar – *la rose du chef.* One evening he came down from the restaurant and said, 'I've got Mireille Matthieu upstairs!' She was a very famous French singer of the time. I knew what he was like, so I asked him, 'Michel, are you sure?'

'Certain!' he said. But I thought I'd better come up and look at her. And sure enough, when I came up I said, 'No, Michel, you are wrong. That's not Mireille Matthieu. It looks like her, but it's not.'

Michel was adamant. 'It is. I'm going to make a rose for her.' So he came down, made the rose, it went upstairs on the plate, and Michel took it to the table and said with a flourish, 'For you, madame.' It didn't go down very well: I really thought the guy who was with that woman was going to thump him. Of course, it was not Mireille Matthieu at all.

Michel played a very big part in Gavroche, and its success belongs to him as well. My brother was a genius. He wouldn't think anything of spending a few hours building up that rose made of sugar. Trying to make him understand how much such a rose costs – that was another matter. I would tell him:

22. In the kitchen with Michel

'My dear friend, you don't go to see the bank, I do. They are not interested in the rose. All they are interested in is the figures, the bottom line.'

'What's that?' would be his reply. Everything Michel did was geared to the art of cooking – he was an artist, and a very clever one at that. His cooking was very precise, with exquisite minute detail. It was all about finesse. But he was not made to open a restaurant, in my view.

I am more instinctive and spur of the moment. I can be precise, but to me it is not the be all and end all. I am more likely to make a decision based on instinct. If I was in the market and saw a bargain on apricots, for example, I would buy not one tray but ten and worry afterwards about what to cook with them. If there's a bargain to be had, let's do it, is my attitude. Michel was more inclined to set things out in detail beforehand.

With Michel and me, our cooking styles were different, and recognisable as different. That is exactly why he got his third Michelin star, and why I got my three stars. When you get to that level, you have your own style, and that's what Michelin recognise. Some know-it-alls used to think they could tell which one of us had cooked a dish. Maybe they could; I certainly always knew if my brother had cooked something, and he knew, vice versa, if I had.

With chefs, there has been a total turnaround, to the despair of the front of the house. In the old days it was all about the maître d'. If you take Maxim's, for example, people would say, 'Shall we go and see Albert, the famous maître d'?'

'Who's the chef there?'

'I don't know, have they got a chef?' In fact, the answer was, the chef is in the basement. If it was four o'clock in the afternoon he was most probably stoned out of his mind drinking and playing cards. And of course there were lots of them, many chefs in every restaurant: again we go back to the long menu, heavy sauces and so forth. People in those days went to restaurants because of the front of house. The front of house was the governor. Now the whole situation is reversed – to their great annoyance, obviously. But they're getting accustomed to it, and they're fighting, amicably, to regain some of their authority. And in the best places, they are succeeding, because I've always taught that good food and good service go hand in hand. It's no good to have one and not the other. It's like the opera: you've got the singer, and you've got the music. Bring them together and you've got a fantastic opera. That has been a problem with our profession. Because it is *our* profession: the success of any restaurant is the harmony which should exist and does exist and is growing between the service and the kitchen. At the Gavroche and our other restaurants, we never made that division, thank God. On the contrary, Michel and I always tried to unify the two. Why? For the benefit of our customers.

This was made easier for us by the arrival at the Gavroche in 1971 of one of the keystones of the restaurant, Silvano Giraldin. Silvano came from the Negresco in France. He applied directly, and I took him on almost as a boy, twenty-two years old, in the role of commis waiter. He worked his way up until, not long afterwards, he became one of the youngest maître d's in the business. Silvano has been a good part of the success of Le Gavroche. He's been with me now for fifty years. He is part of the family.

For me, the most important quality in a maître d' is humility. Humility above all. Even if you're going to look like an idiot to the customer, then look like an idiot. Don't try to outsmart your customer. Many in the up-front profession are show-offs, something which I personally find very embarrassing. Remember that waiter at Maxim's, craning his neck at me and going red in the face because I challenged him? That was the epitome of most service at the time. Humility? Pah! On the contrary, his whole attitude was: 'I'm stronger than you. You should know better than to ask silly questions.' Things can get even worse when it comes to the wine; the wine waiters can really get on my nerves. I've told the sommeliers at the Gavroche: 'When you get to my table, no speech, please. OK, that wine is red, that wine is white? That vine is fifty years old? Well, good luck to it, I hope it lasts another fifty years. But I don't want to hear about it.'

At Le Gavroche, the front of house is there to make the customers feel happy and comfortable. Not to show off in front of them. And Silvano is a master at that.

One of the first jobs I had to do when setting up Le Gavroche was to find the suppliers for the ingredients, because that is where it all starts. For the first year that had to be my job because of Michel's English, which wasn't good enough yet to go to the market and bargain. So my days would start early. The first order of business would be the meat market. Every morning I set out in my van for Smithfield, that vast market like an old train station, with carcasses hung up beneath the enormous wrought-iron rafters, and the whole place smelling of meat and busy with porters in white coats. I did not shop around: when I first went I spent one solid week looking around to see where was the best place to get this or that. Once I had chosen it, by looking at the meat and finding the right trustworthy people, that's where I went. They taught me a lot – how to pick a young lamb, what difference the differing amounts of fat would make. It was the same for the beef and the pork. I was never short of anything, because they trusted me as well. I was a regular; I went there every bloody morning. I wasn't interested in looking for the best price or beating them down in any way, because I knew they would give me the best price for the quality.

The vegetable market was a different thing altogether. It was a cutthroat market, a den of thieves. It was a prehistoric system, heavily unionised. I laugh about it now, but it wasn't always laughable. You had to go and stand under the clock waiting for your porter to be free because you were not allowed to carry things. You knew what was coming up in the lorry from the growers, but only if you were lucky would it end up on the stand. The growers had to send their food to the broker, pay them down, and the broker would ring the farmer at about eleven in the morning, and tell him if he had been successful in sales and at what price. And if he had not been successful, 'Out of my premises!' It was bad in Covent Garden and just as bad when the market moved to Battersea; although the way they ran it all was modernised, it was still the same thing.

The fish came from Billingsgate. That was a joyful market,

a pleasure to be in. Although it was also unionised, it was much more loose. If you wanted to carry your fish, you were welcome, or you put it on the bummaree's head. That place had everything you wanted – amazing fish. It was lovely; I always found it a great delight to do the fish market.

That was my first job every day: get the meat first, then the fish, then last of all vegetables. Once we had established our restaurant in the city, Le Poulbot, I would deliver the meat and the fish there first, then onto the vegetable market and finally deliver it all to Le Gavroche. It would all be put into the *glacière* – in those early days refrigeration came from a big block of ice that was delivered every morning and put underneath the fridge to keep it cold. That ice was a very important delivery.

Michel used to come with me to learn the ropes. It took him about a year to understand the mechanics, and then he was anxious to play a full part. I quite understand that: he wanted not only to do the buying but to take due note of what had to be bought, to take control of it and make the decisions.

These morning tasks would finish about midday; we would change quickly, and get cooking, ready for the evening service – in the early days, the Gavroche wasn't open at lunchtimes. We would meet the chefs and tell them what we had bought for them, and what they were going to do with it. The chefs would have the recipes – they were typed up on an old-fashioned typewriter and kept in neat folders. Each section was expected to follow each recipe precisely, everything exact, right down to the basic dressing for a salad. The ingredients would be weighed out. I would work out the proper way to do everything, and then I would show them: 'Look, just follow me.' Everything should be done properly, in the right fashion. We had to be meticulous; nothing could be left to chance.

The value of the *Le Chef Propose* menu came in at this point, because to some extent it depended on what ingredients we had bought from the markets that day or what the season was. So if we saw a bargain at the market I would snaffle it up and immediately start to think how best to use it. If the vegetable guy offered me a tray of lettuce, for example, I would say, 'OK, but can you do me a better deal if I take two? How many can you sell to me?' So sometimes I would be coming back from the market with ten boxes of an ingredient. Then my mind would get to work, and when I was back in the kitchen I would be saying to the chefs: 'Let's do this: the heart of the lettuce, the very very centre where it is sweetest, we will make a salad. The next layer of leaves we'll make into a soup. The exterior leaves we will blanch and use for staff food.' The food costs would be down because I had been careful about the commodities, and the chefs were expected to use everything. There should be no waste. I hate anything going in the bin; there is no need for it. To put good food in the rubbish is terrible. The thing about those small menus is that it meant everything was fresh: we always finished up in the evening with an empty fridge, so we would start again the next day.

But we found it hard to get some of the supplies we needed in this country. We were a French restaurant and in those days you simply couldn't get quite a lot of the ingredients for the dishes we were trying to cook. In the end, my wife proved to be the solution. Every week she – sometimes with the children – would get into our big Peugeot with a roofrack on top, and drive to a different port – Dover, Folkestone, Southampton. Sometimes she would even take the airplane – in those days you could put your car on an old RAF transporter at Lydd airport. Each time she would change port and change the time of sailing so as not to attract attention. Once in France, she would drive to Paris, to a beautiful shop called Poulet de Bresse, where everything we had ordered from all around Paris would have been delivered and gathered together.

Then she would load the car up: cheese, sausages, fruit and veg, French butter, olive oil, wild mushrooms, truffles, foie gras, real veal. You name it: anything that we couldn't get in England. She would take some produce in the other direction – salmon and grouse. She was our import and export wing. She didn't handle the money side – she was the driver. The car would be crammed full, and she would drive back via a different port each time, hoping that Customs were not going to notice her. If they asked her about her carful of food, she would say 'It's for the family', or 'We are going to have a wedding.' Occasionally she would say, 'Yes, I have something to declare: I bought a pair of shoes.'

On one occasion the sniffer dogs started to get excited, so Customs decided that they would search the car. They took absolutely everything out, and then once everything was out of the car they said, 'OK, we'll put it all back now.' Monique looked innocent and said, 'Oh, they must have been smelling my three dogs that are often in the car with me.' The Customs officers were making faces because they didn't want to handle the produce – the smelly cheeses and the sausages. 'Why didn't you tell us that before we got it all out?' they said.

Perhaps it was because she was a woman, but she never got properly pulled up by Customs. The only time she had real trouble was one time in France. She was coming back with very little in the car at the time, apart from a small amount of wine, and when they asked for her passport and saw from the stamps that she had been to Israel with me a couple of weeks before, they made a huge fuss.

I think Monique found it all a bit nerve-racking. Every time she came back she would say, 'I don't want to do that again, I'm too nervous. You don't realise.' But she did go on doing it, right up until the UK joined the Common Market. And those trips formed the seed for what would become a big part of our business.

We were lucky in that very soon people wanted to work for us and would write to us for jobs. Getting staff at Le Gavroche was never a problem. People would come from all over the world to work there. Our restaurants, especially Le Gavroche and the Waterside Inn, after we opened that up, are thought of as temples of learning. A reference from the Roux restaurants is a very valuable bit of paper. This meant that we could build an excellent team. Over the years at the Gavroche we had a series of high-quality head chefs: Guy Mouilleron, Denis Laubry, Jean-Louis Paul, Jean-Louis Taillebaud, René Bajard, and Steven Doherty. Steven started as a petit commis at the young age of eighteen, and worked his way up to become head chef.

On top of that there are many brilliant chefs who have

worked in the kitchens of Le Gavroche or one of our other restaurants over the years. The list is a long one and contains many names who have contributed a huge amount to our trade: Pierre Koffmann, Gordon Ramsay, Rowley Leigh, Marco Pierre White, Marcus Wareing, Paul Rankin, Bryn Williams, Andrew Fairlie and of course my nephew Alain and my son Michel. Not to mention the hundreds and hundreds of other chefs whose names might not be so well known but have gone on to build their own restaurants and careers. It is a source of great pride to me that these chefs have taken what they learned from the Roux brothers – not just technique but a whole philosophy of hospitality – and spread it far and wide.

And then there was Antonio Batistella, our manager, who had come with the premises, so to speak. He proved to be everything I had predicted he was going to be. Everybody had to love Antonio. He was absent-minded, he had a job recognising people, but he was made to serve, a real treasure. Our relationship was strong for our whole lives, even surviving the moment when I shot him. It was a story that began with our mutual love of shooting, which we had been introduced to by one of our suppliers at Le Gavroche. He had become a good friend and invited Michel and myself to go shooting, which I took to like a duck to water. It suited me down to the ground: I love the countryside, I love dogs and I love game. As did Tony, and we would spend as many Saturdays as we could manage shooting in the morning before returning to the restaurant. One day, in spite of a bit of trouble with my car as I drove up, we had had a successful morning and were invited to extend the shoot onto the land

23. On the steps at Le Gavroche

of a neighbouring farmer. Tony was in the group of beaters, and when the whistle came, he walked into the undergrowth as instructed. Meanwhile I was with the group of guns and, spotting a rabbit coming towards us, I fired. I must have aimed too high, because straight after the sound of my shot I heard a shout ring out. Imagine my horror when I realised I had hit not a rabbit but my friend and employee. Poor Tony: the side of his head and shoulder were peppered with shot and with blood. It was terrifying. Thanks to the swift reactions of one of the other guns, Tony was quickly taken to hospital in Norwich, where they took out as many pellets as possible. To everyone's great relief he was given a clean bill of health by the company doctor on the following Monday, and it did nothing to interfere with our friendship. But I never felt the same about shooting again. I hung up my gun.

At the restaurant, we were busy at weekends, we were busy at night. The family and I were now living in Tooting, in a semi-detached house next to the cemetery, with the four dogs, but I worked all the time. My years at Fairlawne felt like a holiday camp compared to what we went in for with Le Gavroche. But it had been my dream, and it was succeeding.

# 8

## Success

The success of Le Gavroche was simple. We were not in a restaurant, we were still in private service, and the customers to us were like private clients who it was our duty and pleasure to look after. That was the whole intent of the restaurant: it drove everything.

At the Gavroche, we never publicised who had come into the restaurant. We were like Coutts bank: we did not talk about our customers. The press would come to us, saying, 'Mr X was there last night?' To which my answer was, 'If you say so.' We had a shining example of that during the miner's strike, when the president of the Union of Miners in Poland had booked the Waterside for lunch for a big party. And a big party it was; there were about fifty of them in total. It was discreet: there were no photographers, nothing. About a week later, I had a call from a journalist on a national newspaper, asking me to confirm that we had had Mr So-and-So in. I just said, 'If you say so. You are more informed than I am.' But were we open for a party? 'Yes we were, and all I can tell you is they were very happy.' Which they were, and they paid the bill. The journalist didn't want to leave it there, of course. He wanted to know what they had had for their lunch. To which the answer was, 'I can't remember. Whatever they had, they are all still alive and they are all still very happy people. End of story.' The journalist wasn't very pleased though. He said sarcastically, 'Well, you are very cooperative.'

I said, 'Yes, with my clients, yes I am.' And indeed I was.

The truth was that every night there was somebody known to the public in the restaurant. For me, that wasn't unusual; I didn't want to publicise it, and I certainly didn't want to give out their names. That wasn't my job. My job is cooking. Fame has never touched me: I don't think it ever went to my head. I'm very simple. I like to think I'm a friend to everybody. Sometimes the chefs would get overwhelmed: there they were, stuck in a kitchen basement and suddenly they hear a duke or a prince is coming in and everybody's shaking. My attitude is: 'The Queen Mother's coming in? Yes, the Queen Mother's coming in. So what? I expect she needs some food.' I've never been perturbed by things like that, which I think has been part of my strength.

The funny part is that our customers came from every spectrum of society – from the finance world, the political world, the artistic world. We had many famous actors and actresses who would come in time and again: Robert Redford, Yul Brunner, Gregory Peck. There were people from the arts world, from the Rolling Stones to Rudolf Nureyev. Lulu had her wedding reception there when she married one of the Bee Gees. When Charlie Chaplin was a week in London he stayed at the Savoy. Did he eat at the Savoy? Not at all. Every night he came to the Gavroche. He stayed five nights, and had five dinners.

With regulars like that, you don't give them a menu, you know what they want to eat. They always sat at the same table – we made sure of that. There weren't really good and bad tables at Le Gavroche. There were one or two tables which were more discreet, where no one who entered could see you. There were others where nobody could see you at all. When the regulars came in, they didn't ask for a particular table, we just recognised them and took them to their place straight away. That's what makes a great restaurant. Sometimes there were clashes – to sort that out was Silvano's job and he was a master at it. To be able to say to a regular when they were booking, 'Yes, I can book you in, but you can't sit at your regular table because somebody else is there that day.' If you do it in the right way, they will understand. Peter Sellers – who was hugely famous at the time – used to come to the Gavroche often. He always had a particular corner table that he liked, the same one as it happened that our regular customer Andrew Grima usually had. Andrew Grima was jeweller to the Queen and a highly thought of customer who would come in once a week. He called one day to reserve a table, on the same day that Peter Sellers had reserved it. Silvano spoke to him and said, 'Look, Mr Grima, I'm sorry sorry sorry but I have Peter Sellers on that table. Of course I can give you a booking but it will have to be at a different table.'

24. The visitors' book at Le Gavroche

'Hmmmm,' said Mr Grima. 'Well, he had better have a prettier girl than me!'

The Queen Mother came often. She always had the same thing – the *Soufflé Suissesse*. She would never call it that; she would say, 'Can you tell the chef I want my soufflé?' Princess Diana came quite a lot as well. Lord Attenborough – Richard Attenborough – would bring her every couple of weeks, and they were always seated at the same table – one that was quite discreet. She loved it there – she must have come at least twenty times. I remember her coming up the stairs one day and catching sight of the portrait of me being named professor at the University of Bournemouth (they gave me the honour because of my work with developing sous vide techniques with them). 'Yes,' she said jokingly, 'I tell you – he is the Professor of Spaghetti.'

We had no journalists, no photographers; we discouraged them, and tried not to be the sort of place where they hung around outside. This was easier in Lower Sloane Street – when we moved to the new premises in Upper Brook Street there were a couple of times where we had to tell the client that there were photographers outside, and to ask them if they wanted to use a private entrance. There were three private entrances there. I remember very clearly at five or six in the evening there would often be photographers waiting outside getting soaked. And the person they were aiming at had long gone home.

Princess Diana was a magnet to them. They would be lined up outside. On one occasion, we went to tell her the press were outside, and asked whether she would like to use the private entrance. 'Ah,' she said, 'let's face them.' And she went

**25. At work with Michel**

out the front door. That was her choice. It was not for me to say 'you mustn't . . .'

There is a picture of one day, when she came out of the Gavroche to a pack of press and she pushed away the driver saying, 'I'm going to drive.' She stormed away. On one occasion – around the time that the book about her by Andrew Morton came out – she heard the paparazzi were outside and turned to Silvano. 'You called them!' she said. Silvano didn't even answer – it was so clearly not true. The press knew everything about her: where she was, where she slept. But that was Diana – the story of her life.

Because we were known to be discreet and trustworthy, it started very quickly to buzz, and for people to say, 'It's pretty safe to go there with your mistress.' I remember clearly table number one, which was in the alcove at the new Gavroche. That was one of the more secret tables, and was often used for that purpose. One evening there was a couple who had booked – a beautiful woman, and a very nicely dressed gentleman. We sent up their first course, and they had it, and then there was a long pause. Ten minutes, fifteen minutes went by. I was wondering, when were they going to call for the next course? It turned out the lady and the gentleman had gone to the toilet . . . the thing is, they had gone to the same toilet together, the ladies. Silvano kept quite calm – he straight away marked the toilet as out of order, and left a waiter up front, saying, 'Nobody is to enter this room until those two people come out.' It took a while: they came out fifteen or twenty minutes later. The gentleman said thank you to Silvano and discreetly put out his hand and gave him a handful of notes.

You would see all sorts at the Gavroche. I remember one time we had a man who came in with his mistress, and at the same time on the same day his wife came in with her toyboy. They both had their meal, and acknowledged each other before they went on their way. 'Well,' I said to Silvano. 'Fine by me. Let them both pay.' But we were not surprised to hear a few months later that they were divorcing.

There was another occasion with one customer who regularly used to bring his mistress to the Gavroche. One day his son and daughter-in-law had booked a table. When the old man arrived with his mistress as usual, Silvano happened to be at the front door. 'No,' said Silvano, 'I will not let you in today.'

'Harrumph', said the man arrogantly.

So Silvano took him aside quietly: 'Your son is having dinner downstairs – he didn't book under his own name, he booked under his wife's. So, what do you want to do? Would you like to come in?' The man scarpered pretty quickly. We had a lot of that kind of thing, but we never said anything. As Silvano would say, you could talk about the sin, but never the sinner.

Anybody was welcome at the Gavroche, but if they misbehaved, then out they would go on the spot. I would send them on their way myself. I had one or two situations like that, where somebody's behaviour wasn't OK. I would usually wait until the end of their meal before saying anything.

'Can I have a taxi?' they would say.

I would be polite: 'The taxi is at the door.'

Then – 'Can I have the bill?'

To which I would say. 'Don't worry about it, it's a gift,

but please do not come back.' That was it for them, as far as I was concerned.

I remember one particular evening, where one of the customers whistled to call the waiter. The minute I heard about this, I left what I was doing in the kitchen and went upstairs. I made sure the taxi had been called, and then I went over to the customer and said 'Sir, your taxi is outside.'

He was there with a lady, I remember that. He said, 'But I haven't asked for the bill'.

I said, 'No, there is no bill, you are my guest. Now, your taxi is outside.'

He was not pleased. He started trying to throw his weight around, telling me how important he was. But I said, 'Do not behave like that in public places. If you need a waiter, call for a waiter, don't whistle. We've got no dogs here.'

'Oh.' he said. Then: 'Let me give you the money.'

I still remember what I said to him: 'Absolutely not. Money is not everything. Money is not manners. You haven't got any.'

The Cazalets had plenty of dogs, they were lovers of dogs. They might have whistled for the dogs, but I never heard them whistle when they wanted to talk to me. They called the butler to come and see them, or me to come and see them, or they came to see me. I was not going to have my staff whistled at, and I was not afraid to tell that man so.

Now, it could have been a disaster to talk to a customer in that way. I recognise that. But it wasn't. And I was not going to put up with that kind of behaviour in my restaurant.

# 9

## New Enterprises

With the Gavroche up and running, all was well. We were
full every day. But I am an entrepreneur and I am always
looking for new ventures. So after a while I came across the
opportunity to open Le Poulbot – another urchin – on the site
of an old pub in Cheapside. This was in 1969. On the ground
floor we kept the pub style and served more modestly priced
food, and downstairs was a smart restaurant. Rowley Leigh
was the head chef there for many years. We did it up in red
with high-backed booths and it felt very luxurious. It felt a bit
like a club, and the booths made it very private because you
could have a conversation in them and nobody would hear.
It would be open for five days a week, right in the middle of
the City. We served both breakfast and lunch, but not dinner,
which was revolutionary at the time. It was always full
as well.

After that, we decided to open a delicatessen, Le Cochon

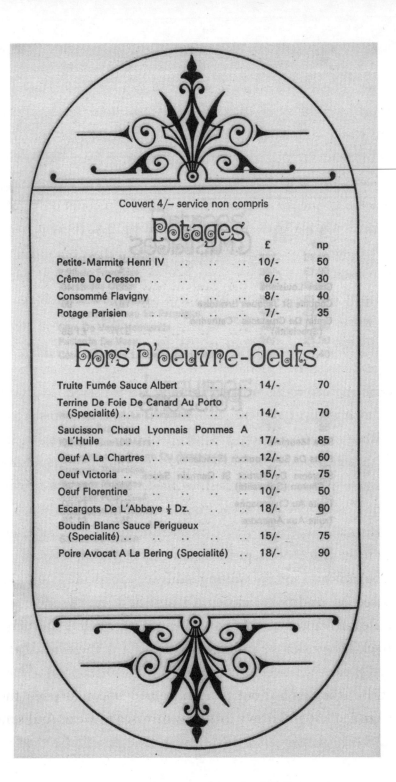

Couvert 4/– service non compris

## Potages

| | £ | np |
|---|---|---|
| Petite-Marmite Henri IV .. .. .. | 10/- | 50 |
| Crême De Cresson .. .. .. .. | 6/- | 30 |
| Consommé Flavigny .. .. .. | 8/- | 40 |
| Potage Parisien .. .. .. | 7/- | 35 |

## Hors D'oeuvre-Oeufs

| | £ | np |
|---|---|---|
| Truite Fumée Sauce Albert .. .. | 14/- | 70 |
| Terrine De Foie De Canard Au Porto (Specialité) .. .. .. .. .. | 14/- | 70 |
| Saucisson Chaud Lyonnais Pommes A L'Huile .. .. .. .. .. | 17/- | 85 |
| Oeuf A La Chartres .. .. .. | 12/- | 60 |
| Oeuf Victoria .. .. .. .. | 15/- | 75 |
| Oeuf Florentine .. .. .. | 10/- | 50 |
| Escargots De L'Abbaye ½ Dz. .. .. | 18/- | 90 |
| Boudin Blanc Sauce Perigueux (Specialité) .. .. .. .. .. | 15/- | 75 |
| Poire Avocat A La Bering (Specialité) .. | 18/- | 90 |

26.  An early menu from Le Poulbot

Rose, a couple of doors down from Le Gavroche. I brought over my elder sister, Liliane, to run it with her husband Paul. He was a very talented charcutier – a wonderful craftsman at his trade. It still was at the time the only place in London besides one shop in Soho where you could buy garlic sausage, black pudding, *choucroute*, all the things you could only get in France. We had the best salami, the best pâtés, the best meats. An amazing charcuterie. We got David Mlinaric in again to decorate it – he made it look fantastic with blue-and-white-striped awnings and a big space inside for the charcutier to work.

In 1971 we opened the Brasserie Benoit. (We called it that because Benoit had been our grandfather's name). Our concept here was a brasserie in the Alsacien style; it was very French, and very different to everything else that was around at the time. We would do *choucroute* and other regional dishes, with huge glasses of Alsacien beer on tap. It was another basement, this time with a great magnificent staircase, which you descended and came into an enormous space with a beautiful mosaic floor. We broke it up with wall partitions to make it look less gigantic, and there was a fabulous bar. The uniforms for the waiting staff were particularly unusual, based on traditional clothing from the area: the men were in leather aprons and the women in huge white shirts and thick heavy skirts in different colours. On their heads they had great big black Alsacien coifs. They were fantastic to look at. But they turned out to be extremely uncomfortable: they were too hot and heavy for the waitresses to wear. And some of the food turned out not to be totally practical either, not

27. Staff at Brasserie Benoit

to mention that in the City in those days things were dead after the working day so there was no reason to open at night. After a while we decided to simplify the place: we kept the things that were working and Brasserie Benoit became Le Gamin – one more urchin for the family. As Le Gamin it was open at lunchtime only and it was packed. It was all super-fast service, packing them in, and became a huge success.

The other thing that arose from that was the contract catering side. Having been invited a few times to the City by grandees, I became used to the kind of food you could get at the smart companies there. The food was disgusting; as soon as you got out of the taxi, you could already sniff the overboiled cabbage. There were also sandwich bars which would deliver to businesses, but it was very basic stuff. Once Brasserie Benoit had opened, we realised we had an opportunity because we had these huge kitchens right in the heart of the right area, near the Old Bailey. So we started delivering food – really just takeaway stuff at first, but good quality braised lamb or roast beef – to merchant banks and other companies that needed their directors' lunches. The enterprise grew and grew. The menu changed daily, and they had a choice; they would ring in the morning to order, and we would deliver it all ready to be reheated. We would do the deliveries between eleven and twelve in the morning – all the offices were situated in the Square Mile so it wasn't too hard to get to them all, but it was still busy. In the early days, one guy would be driving the van, and another would take the boxes out and literally run down the street delivering them. Usually the banks employed ladies – and occasionally butlers – to look after the directors, and they would have little Belling ovens to keep the food warm and dish it up on plates.

Our first client was stockbroking firm Grieveson Grant, where we managed to dislodge Prue Leith, unfortunately, who had the contract there before us. I'm very friendly with Prue; I've got a great admiration for her and a lot of time. She is very clever, but I'm afraid she lost the contract there. After a while we put a permanent chef there on a contract basis. It was pioneering at the time – now it has become more usual as a practice.

Tony Batistella – the wonderful manager who had been with Gavroche since before the start – was put in charge of the outside catering, and he kept it running to a high standard. We delivered to the banks Monday to Friday for their lunches, and then in the evenings we might do canapés for any functions they were holding. We would provide the food and the service because we had all the waiting staff from the restaurant, which was by then only open at lunchtime, who could go on working into the evening. It then widened out into weekends and special events, and became a big part of the business.

Tony used to tell the story of how one day a newish customer at one of the stockbrokers asked him in to talk about the menus, complaining that all the sauces on the different meat dishes tasted exactly the same. This was very strange – Tony knew the chef had been working properly and that the sauces for the dishes should be perfect – thick and full of flavour. So the next time a delivery was made, he followed it to the dining room, and discovered that the waitress was just about to drain the meat of its sauce and replace it with watery gravy made with granules from a tin that she carried about with her. As far as she was concerned, our sauces were too thick and there wasn't enough of them. She felt these big important businessmen needed a proper amount of gravy, so she had taken it into her own hands and 'fixed' the problem. I think Tony was lost for words.

It was also being around those city types that led us to search outside London for our next restaurant, because I realised that all those grand sorts of people lived around Ascot and would love to be able to have a first-class restaurant nearby. Hence the birth of the Waterside Inn, the other jewel in our crown. It was a beautiful spot on the banks of the Thames in Bray. It had been an old pub, and when we got it the place still had that old pub smell – tobacco and beer stains on the carpet, and a wall blocking any views of the river. But we made it beautiful. Michel had always wanted a country restaurant and now we had one. We worked out that we would each do one week at the Gavroche and one week at the Waterside.

About six or seven years after starting Le Gavroche, it was still only open in the evenings, and we decided there could be a business at lunchtime also. We came to the conclusion that the best way to do it would be to have a *prix-fixe* menu, for which I was laughed at by the trade. In those days there was lunch only in hotels – people thought of it as a decadent kind of thing: a whole rigamarole with cigars and port, finishing at five in the evening. There was to my knowledge nothing like what we were planning to open: somewhere that people could come and get a high-quality meal in the middle of their day. That's why the trade laughed and asked what I was up to. It just wasn't done. I had the last laugh, though, because lunchtime went from being a no man's land to being very busy. We started to attract a new clientele: taxi drivers, hairdressers, hardworking people, professionals who couldn't afford to come in the evening. But the main thing was that the *prix-fixe* was not lesser quality, it was not the leftovers. It was well-prepared, well costed, with good ingredients. We still offer the *prix-fixe* at lunchtime, and it is interesting to see that 75 per cent of the customers at lunchtime have it. But of course it only made us more busy.

Then there was Boucherie Lamartine – this was an extension of the import business that had started up with Monique driving to France. The boucherie was the talk of the town in Pimlico: it was the best food from France – a *traiteur*, butcher and grocer's shop combined. We had fantastic customers; there were queues of people round the block because the quality was so good and you couldn't get those ingredients anywhere else. We supplied other restaurants too. I put Marc Beaujeu, a charcutier turned chef who had been with the company almost from the start, in charge. The shop looked wonderful: on the outside it was painted black and cream with wrought iron. There were windows full of racks of meat. Inside, there were freezers and shelves of the best ingredients. It was so successful that we ended up opening other branches in Covent Garden and near the Connaught hotel.

I always enjoyed looking for the next thing to do, and I loved having new ideas. Michel, on the other hand, was invariably

28.  Boucherie Lamartine

29. Inside Boucherie Lamartine

against opening other restaurants. To me, learning has always been an ongoing process. As soon as you say, 'I've done it', there's only one way to go: down. I am an entrepreneur and a gambler, because every entrepreneur is a gambler. It was certainly not true that everything I did was successful: it was not. I had my failures, but on the other hand I survived.

In 1974 Le Gavroche was awarded a Michelin star – the first star to be awarded in the UK. To tell the truth, that first Michelin star did not mean a huge amount to me. At that time the Michelin was associated with older restaurants which were not really the calibre we were aiming at. Nowadays, the Michelin has evolved – it follows the feedback from their customers but in those days it was a bit different. Nevertheless, it was a great accolade, especially when that first star was followed in 1977 by a second one: now we were the first two-star restaurant in the country.

In 1981 we had a big change, deciding to move Le Gavroche from its home in Lower Sloane Street to Upper Brook Street. It was a practical thing: the main reason we moved was to get more space – more space in the rooms, more space overall. The Lower Sloane Street restaurant limited us in size – it was cosy in a way but there was no possibility to extend it. There was no space for the bar, or for a separate cash desk or cloakroom. The wine had to be stored under the banquettes that the customers were sitting on. In the new place we would have more room to grow, and the kitchen would be level with the restaurant, which was very important to us. The waiters and the chefs would no longer have to work in the basement. They would be able to see daylight, or half daylight at least.

No more sweltering heat or opening up the escape hatch to let some air in. Above all, no more argy-bargy over the dumb waiters. All in all, the new Gavroche was a better environment, and a better fit for the customers we attracted. It was a risk though, no doubt about it: there was a lot of planning, a lot of hard work and a huge investment. It meant going from a smallish team in the kitchen and front of house to a larger one, so we were recruiting and getting everyone firing on all cylinders. The feel of the new place was similar to the old one though the décor was different – now it was rich greens and the walls hung with many pictures. But it retained the feeling of a private establishment.

There was no doubt a risk in moving, in uprooting our successful establishment and transplanting it elsewhere. But there is always a risk in anything. You make a decision that by changing something it is going to work better, but of course you are taking a gamble. That is in my nature – they call me a risktaker, which I am. Opening Gavroche in the first place was a huge gamble, though it might not look like it now.

This particular risk ended up reaping a big reward, which was 47 Park Street. This was the hotel above the restaurant, with its entrance round the corner. It was owned by Berndt Nigram, a Swedish man who bought it at about the same time that we moved in. We hit it off as friends, I did a deal with him and we entered into a business partnership. This meant I got to run it as a hotel the way I wanted. After looking at what was missing for the businessman traveller – and for tourists – I figured out that what they wanted most was space. That, and large ensuite bathrooms. Some businessmen seem to spend more time in the bathroom than they do in their beds. This sounds run of the mill now, but it wasn't then. I had a vision for the hotel; Monique helped with the décor, and it was a big part of its success. I wanted to make it a high-end luxury place, but like the restaurant, I wanted it to have the feel of a private establishment. So nearly every room was different – that was what made it special, and it was very unusual then. In most hotels everything was uniform.

All of this was pooh-poohed by the industry – they thought each room should be exactly the same and that it should be done up like everywhere else. I remember Rocco Forte coming to have a look out of interest. His words were: 'You're mad. It will never work.' Perhaps two years later, two floors of the Grosvenor became ensuite, trying to be like mine. By then we were flying. Park Street was the most successful business I ever had. Occupancy was touching 85 per cent all year round. Our repeat clients ran at 70 per cent. People used to come from New York by Concorde, go home for the weekends, and come back on Mondays. The room was still there to let – if I was clever, I used to let it for the weekend. We became part of the Relais Chateaux group, and ended up selling it to a French company, nine years after opening, for a huge profit.

After the move to Upper Brook Street, we kept the old Lower Sloane Street site on, and opened Gavvers there – this was a bit like Le Gamin in idea and style, but maybe more high end. Again, it featured regional specialities: *beef bourgignon,* roast chicken. French provincial-style food, but presented in a more sophisticated way than you would in the brasserie.

In 1982, Le Gavroche was awarded a third Michelin star.

This was acclaimed to be huge news: we were the first three-Michelin-star restaurant in the country. The press talked and talked about it, and we even made it to *Time* magazine. Getting that star was certainly a surprise, because I did not cook for the likes of Michelin. I have always maintained, and still do, that I cook for the customer. If the Michelin Guide says the restaurant is worth three stars, well fine, let's have those stars. But it is not my decision, and it will not change the way that I run my restaurant, or the principles that the restaurant will be guided by. Saying that, I was delighted to receive it, mostly if not entirely because of the workforce. They had worked so hard, and been so dedicated. So for that reason the achievement was wonderful. The Michelin has always been the place for restaurants to be mentioned, let alone get the star. It's a reference book for chefs and customers, and it is very hard to achieve. And there is no doubt it can make a huge difference to a chef's life. Look at Gordon Ramsay – a dear friend and a great talent who has had a wonderful career.

But for me, there was still more to do. I was always fascinated to see what the next thing was. In the early eighties, I became very interested in the art of sous vide cooking, which was already a big thing in France. I thought this was cutting-edge technology – it could be useful not just in restaurant cooking but in catering and even at home. I saw it as a way to ensure good consistent quality in bulk catering, for events or schools or institutions. So I brought vacuum packing into the Gavroche kitchen in the early 1980s, and we were one of the first kitchens to have a vacuum pack machine. I sent Steven Doherty, our head chef, and also my son, Michel, to a course in France to learn all about the different techniques of conservation, pasteurisation, sterilisation and the best ways to cook meat and fish and vegetables. We set up the Rouxl Britannia restaurants – restaurants that would rely on sous vide – and also launched a home range with Marks and Spencer. I thought it had the capacity to be something great, and we spent a lot of time and energy on it. We also spent money – we built a whole factory dedicated to it. But we were too ahead of our time. It was too early, and just didn't take off in the way we hoped as far as home cooking went. In France you can go into Carrefour and there are rows of sous vide products. But the British public didn't take to it in the same way. Having said that, it is now standard in every restaurant kitchen. It has transformed cooking, and that is partly because of all the chefs who came through the Gavroche kitchens and embraced it and took the technique on with them. Chefs look at it now and think of it as technology, but we were doing it forty years ago.

In all of these enterprises, I was always the driver. My brother would have preferred to do one thing well and keep doing it. After about sixteen years, I realised things were coming to a point with us that if we kept going there would be a bust-up between us. He had always looked up to me as the older brother, but he had his own ideas. He had grown, his English had improved, he had his family here, and he understood the business side. We realised it was time to separate. So we split the business. There were two crown jewel restaurants – Le Gavroche and the Waterside Inn. I asked Michel which of them he would prefer, and he said he would prefer to go to the country. I said fine. So the Waterside Inn became his, and I stayed at the Gavroche. No money was exchanged: it was an amicable split. We gave each other a kiss, and that was it: we went our separate ways.

Looking back, I have been asked again and again, was it good to be associated with your brother for so long? Invariably, the answer is no, and yet the answer is yes. We had seventeen years together, which is a long time in the starting and moulding of a business. Was he an integral part of it all? Of course, yes. He was a maniac in some ways, and a pain the arse. This could be a good thing: he was very demanding about standards, very strict, which was extremely helpful. You can still see it in the Waterside today – it's a perfect establishment, every detail in place. But would I want to work again with my brother? No. It might be a hard thing to say, but it does not denigrate in any way what he achieved.

As a brother, he was always precious to me. But we did not always agree, especially in business. I am what I would call a forcible man in my ideas: as far as I am concerned, you have to do what I think, and if you don't want to do that, you need to tell me the reasons why. If you can persuade me, then I might change my mind. But I can see that this might have been difficult for my brother. He was an artist, far more than I am or will ever be. He was a hard worker, an extreme professional, and he has proved it by being a huge success in his own right. That is something that makes me highly delighted and proud. But, as my mother used to call him, he was also 'Mr Critic'. He used to criticise everything throughout his whole life, but he didn't like to be criticised himself, not at all. So after seventeen years together I could feel I had an unhappy brother, who wanted to fly his own kite. That is normal. There was no resentment: our professional association lasted all that time, but it had to come to an end for both our sanity, both his and mine.

So the Waterside went to him, and Le Gavroche stayed with me. We put the other ventures – Le Poulbot, the other restaurants, the outside catering – into another company and raised money for that. Unfortunately around that time the financial crash came, and we found ourselves not exactly in difficulty, but in a situation where the money we were making on the successful ventures was beginning to subsidise those places that were left behind. It was rather a sad moment, so we decided to sell out, and pay back the people who had put money into them.

Le Poulbot had a long lease, fifty years with no review, so it was a valuable property. I had a very large offer of money from McDonald's when we put it on the market. The governor of the Bank of England, who owned the freehold of the property, was horrified to think there could be a McDonald's inside the premises. They had the right on the lease to oppose it, because it had a lot of small print. So eventually we sold it to a building society, and finished up by making good money on it. This still left us with another three restaurants which we could not dispose of. There were no takers because of the recession, so we had to close them. It was a sad moment, but we survived.

The outside catering company – Roux Fine Dining – was still a huge success throughout all this. One day, during Ascot week, I was at the races. When I went into the gent's, there was a tall guy next to me. 'Hello, Albert,' he said. I said hello. He introduced himself as Francis McKay of Compass Group, who had just done a management buyout of a firm of contract caterers. He said, 'I would like to meet up with you, to see if there is synergy between your business and my business. I would be interested in doing a deal.'

So appointments were made, several meetings took place, and after about six months the deal was closed. It had come at the right time. I stayed on as a consultant for Compass and have been with them ever since.

# 10

# Food in my Life

Cooking has always been in my brain. I start with being concerned about ingredients. To me that is primordial. The taste of good ingredients depends on their origins: that's related to the garden and the farm. That's why I used to take such an interest in the gardeners at Fairlawne and why I have always grown my own vegetables.

With the restaurants, from the moment I got out of bed and went to the market and saw the food there, I would be thinking. I would see the meat with the butcher, and I would translate it into the pan, and then I would translate it onto the plate, and then I would translate it into a happy customer. So the brain starts with the ingredients. It starts when I go into the fields and see the farmer and the cultivator who bring those foods to the market. That's why I went to the Amazon, for example. I spent several weeks there with an ice cream machine looking at wild fruit and making ice cream. The tastes of those fruits are still in my mind: they are spectacular. Take the wild mango; at the time I was working for Marks and Spencer – I spent twenty years with M&S developing new dishes and also talking to them about ingredients. The mango was one of those fruits that took quite a time to hit the nail. But it hit the nail because in the end they are what the customer wants. It's a long slog, to give a new ingredient to the public and to try and get them familiar with it. It's interesting, because when you introduce the mango, and put it in the hand of a would-be customer, it looks like a grenade – is it going to explode? And indeed it did: its flavour exploded into their mind and they decided that they wanted it.

I don't invent dishes. That is a word that is widely used by chefs, but it's wrong. To innovate, yes and mix things up, and hopefully come up with something unique. That happens once in a thousand years, then you have a big winner. Do I know when a dish is perfect? Well, yes and no, because first of all you have to like what you're doing. You are the ultimate judge of whether you have something great or not. The second judge, for lack of a better word, is the customer: if they like it too, then you are on to something. That was why our *Chef Propose* menu was useful – it was where we could try things out. It helped us to judge with a new dish whether it was worth carrying on, or needed to be developed further, or whether we should abandon it.

As for inspiration, I travelled a lot, not just throughout Europe but throughout the world. And while I was travelling, where did I spend my time? I visited markets and I visited restaurants – museums will have to wait for another time.

I missed those. I also read a lot – I read all sorts of things, but there are certain cookery books and authors that I revere. Escoffier, of course. And Édouard Nignon, a contemporary of Escoffier: his books were also bibles to me. He talked about the philosophy of taste and cooking as well as recipes. I collect old cookery books, and old menus as well. I find them fascinating.

There are some dishes I am still very proud of. The *Soufflé Suissesse* is still on the menu at Gavroche. It is a beautiful dish – two soufflés that are baked quickly, then rebaked in a dish of cream with three different types of cheeses. It has always been one of our most popular starters. At the other end of the menu is the *Omelette Rothschild* – a sweet omelette soufflé, made in an omelette pan and glazed with apricot jam. It is delicious. It is still on the menu too – it has changed slightly, but every ingredient is from the original recipe. The *pot au feu sauce Albert* is one of my absolute favourite main courses – I love *pot au feu* and there is no reason why a staple like this cannot be elevated to three-star level. That is the heart of what we do. That dish was on our first menu and encapsulates a lot of what our cooking is about. *Rognons de Veau aux Trois Moutardes. Cotes d'Agneau a l'estragon. Homard a l'Escargot. Les Huitres Francine. Mousseline de Homard au Champagne.* All of these take prime ingredients and highlight them by cooking them to absolute perfection, staying faithful to the techniques of classic French cooking.

There was the odd dish that didn't work. Not through lack of skill or care in the kitchen, but because they didn't quite suit. One day I put on a dish called *oeufs Muscovite*. I took a soft-boiled egg, cut the top off, emptied everything out and mixed it with caviar. It was wonderful. But it had to be served warm and had to be cooked almost *à la minute*. The first time we put it on the *Chef Propose* menu, Silvano sold it to the first five or six customers who came in. Then it was chaos to try and get them all out at the right time. I did not do that dish again. But that sort of thing was rare – we considered very carefully what we were putting on the menu. Running a successful restaurant – like running anything – is all to do with mistakes. You analyse what went wrong, and then you change things or don't change them. But you have to pay attention. If we had not ascertained properly the causes of the mistakes that we made, we would not be here today. It's simple arithmetic. You got it wrong? Well, don't do it again. In the kitchen, you should celebrate mistakes, so long as they are mistakes that you correct. If you can decipher what happened during the chain of the mistake you become stronger. That is the key.

Certain dishes I did could be described as controversial. Like tripe, for example. Regardless of what you do to it, whether you add caviar to it or anything, it is still tripe. I am very fond of it, though I can't have it on a daily basis. It is hard to get people to appreciate it, though it has become more fashionable lately. Some experiments that seem daring do catch on. I did a dish which was cod's liver – I like cod's liver – and I thought it would be nice to add foie gras to it and I was right: it became extremely popular.

The style of eating has changed a lot since we started. People's tastes have evolved, and demand has grown. Obviously you cook something to sell it for the pleasure of the customer. If – and of course it happens – you get a negative response from the customer, you stop doing it. There's no point trying to be more scientific than they are: the customer is king.

One thing I have been very lucky with is that I love to teach, and I have had the opportunity. When I was coming up in my profession I was fortunate that there were some older people who were willing to show me their secrets, how to do this, how to do that, who were not mean with their time or their expertise. I certainly have met more than a few mean people in the kitchen in my life, people who hid themselves away when they were doing something, saying 'Go pluck the pigeons' if you asked to be shown anything. I cannot understand that. To me there is nothing more rewarding than teaching, and being generous with your knowledge. Nowadays I get letters from all over the world: 'Chef, if you are ever in Kuala Lumpur, I just landed a top job, thank you for all I learned when I spent time working for you.' That's the rewarding part of what I do: it's the fruit. I like to think that after anyone has worked for me I am there for them as a mentor and a guide. I try to be always available at the end of a phone – they can give me a call and I will listen.

That is one of the reasons my brother Michel and I set up the Roux Scholarship. This was an idea that came about in 1984, originally with the support of Diners Club International, to develop and nurture chefs and encourage classic French techniques. It is one of the toughest cooking competitions there is, and rightly so, because the prize is invaluable – the chance to cook at any three-Michelin-star restaurant of their choice, and incidentally to have forever the support of the Roux family. (Nowadays, Michel and I have passed the judging duties on to our sons, Alain and Michel Jr.) The first winner was Andrew Fairlie, who went on to have his own two-star restaurant in Scotland. The Roux scholars over the years have gone right to the top of the profession, and I am fantastically proud of them and of the competition.

I have also been very lucky in that I have been recognised for the work I have done: in this country, I have been given an OBE. In France, I was given the Chevalier de Légion d'Honneur. I have multiple achievement awards, and was even awarded a papal knighthood. I am very proud of all of them. But what makes me most proud are the chefs I have helped to train, and the way that they have gone out and done great things in the world of cooking. That I think is the legacy of the Roux brothers, and I attribute that to the way that we taught them.

Unfortunately what we see too often is the habit and the language of diminishing people in front of others. There is nothing worse than that. I can't stand to see people belittling and discouraging those poor boys and girls whose only wish is to learn. I don't allow that, just as I don't allow swearing or pushing in my kitchens. Obviously, if people cannot learn, I don't employ them for long. But I am merciful about it. My way of doing it is: 'Come into my office. Have a beer, or a glass of champagne. Let's have a drink. Now, you are not fit as yet to work in the environment that I am providing you. Does that make you a lesser person? No, of course not.' There is no need to attack their character: that used to be how cooking was, but there is no need for it. One person might take two hours to peel a bag of potatoes; another person might take a day. So yes, the first one is more efficient. But the other one is not a lesser person, he just needs to learn how to handle potatoes in a proper manner. You do not attack his personality for that. People need attention and care, and that way you can make a racehorse out of a donkey as I like to say. We have lost some very talented boys and girls, who could have done better if they had been treated properly. It is known in the trade that I am a glutton for punishment, and always like to give people another chance.

Nothing pains me more than seeing an average brigade of chefs in an average restaurant, maybe with ten or twelve people, who are not working properly together. Success is to make them gel and complement each other. In other words, nobody should be fighting against what the other people are doing. There is nothing better in teaching than to show these young people that this is possible. The first question is, are they dedicated to what they are doing? I like to have anyone in my kitchen who is dedicated and wants to learn. I was the first Michelin-starred chef to employ a woman in the kitchen. Other chefs laughed at me at the time. But if you asked them all where they learned to cook and why, it was from their grandmothers, or their mothers. Actually, I have found that women often have more stamina. They do not get as tired as the men do. They are often more artistic in their presentation. It isn't nearly so hard nowadays for a woman to break into the profession. But the work now is not so physical as it was: saucepans are much lighter, the size of flour sacks is smaller.

Equipment has changed so that things are less heavy and difficult to manoeuvre. And the hours are not so bad as they were, although in the hospitality industry there will always be long and antisocial shifts. But there is perhaps now more understanding in the workplace; kitchens are also not as masculine and hostile as in the old days. I like to think we had something to do with that. I am proud of my profession, and I want it to be open to anyone with talent.

~

By 1991 I had been running the Gavroche for twenty-four years, six of them on my own. By now, my son Michel was working as a manager at Le Poulbot, having done his pâtisserie apprenticeship in Paris and worked all over the world, including in the Élysées Palace for his military service, at Alain Chapel's three-star restaurant in Mionnay, near Lyons, and at the Mandarin Hotel in Hong Kong. He had found his own way in life and had experiences all over the world. Back in London, he gained experience at Gavvers, Le Gamin and the private catering side of the company, as well as at Le Poulbot. In about 1988 he joined me in Le Gavroche. At around this time I began to feel that I wanted to move on. So eventually we came to an agreement and I handed over the reins to him.

There was no question of me retiring: I like to work. But this freed me up to take on new challenges, such as the Chez Roux restaurants – we have a number of them, particularly in my beloved Scotland. I love Scotland for the nature there, and for the people, both are fantastic. I opened up Bertie's, in Paris – a chance to go in the other direction and bring British cooking to the French. There have been consultancies with everyone from Concorde to Marks and Spencer and ICMI. And opportunities to lecture and to teach, which I love to do.

Unfortunately the demands of being a restaurateur can be harmful to family life – through the years when I was so busy with the restaurants, working like a madman at Le Gavroche, Poulbot, Waterside and all the others, Monique and I were too much apart. We had bought a beautiful country house in Petworth within a year of opening Le Gavroche. It had everything you could want: space, countryside, animals – it was almost like a mini farm. But I think Monique was lonely there, because I was in London all the time, returning on Sundays only to sleep, really. And I must admit that I was not always the ideal husband. This sadly led to the end of our marriage in 2001, though we remained good friends. My second marriage did not end quite so happily. But then I met my wife Maria, and found joy again.

There have been opportunities to take stock in other ways. About twenty-two years ago I was in Geneva where I had charge of a little bijou hotel called L'Hotel d'Angleterre. The director of the hotel introduced me to an elegant lady who turned out to be Princess Margarita, who would have been the heir to the throne of Romania had her father not had to forcibly abdicate. She was looking for help with an orphanage she was starting in her home country. This was around the time that the scandals of the Romanian orphanages under Ceausescu had been discovered, and she and her husband Radu

155

30. Returning to Charolles with my mother

were trying to do what they could. She was totally dedicated to the plight of those children – what she did is incredible: building them special houses, teaching them, making sure that when they grew up they had a decent job. I found her a fascinating woman, so I offered to help. I raised money, very successfully, by giving a black-tie dinner with an auction in Gavroche one evening, and then we repeated it in the hotel in Switzerland, and again in Amsterdam where I had another large hotel. All of this raised several million pounds for the charity. Because of this I visited Romania a couple of times a year. It was quite an eye-opener to me because here was someone who did not have a lot of money herself, though she was very well connected – her godfather was Prince Philip. But she was nevertheless dedicating herself to this cause. She kindly gave me the highest decoration she could give – the Order of the Crown of Romania – at a special black-tie event in the old Bank of Romania.

All of this work with her charity led me to think profoundly about my life, and I found I was suddenly thinking again about faith, because although I had cut myself off from the Church I would still consider myself a man of faith. That was the moment when I realised that what happened to me as a child with that dirty stinking priest was not what the Church was about. I had already started to consider this back in Tonbridge when I got married, but it was now that I realised that, wrongly, I had identified that dirty old priest with Jesus himself. Over the years I came to realise that this was incorrect; that *curé*, that dirty stinking man, was nothing but a waiter, serving a meal. He was not the boss! He was an employee who should not have been doing what he was doing. And he was a bad waiter. I run public places, and if you go to one of my restaurants expecting something special and the waiter spills soup on you or says something rude, then you quite rightly come out very disappointed. And you will pass a judgement, perhaps on me. But that waiter, he's not me, and he's not the restaurant. Don't start blaming the Almighty because one of the servants has behaved badly.

In my mind I gradually realised that though I was blaming the whole of the Church, the institution was not all like that; among their number there were also some very dedicated priests. Not all of them were bad. I had not been able to see that at the time, but now I was witnessing it in action. So I started to think a little differently. There is no doubt that terrible things have happened in the Church in too many countries – Ireland, America, France. It is very sad. There are far too many bad waiters. But I reconciled myself to it, a little bit.

I remain on the board of Le Gavroche, of course. The style, when Michel took over, remained the same. He didn't change the spirit of the place, bless him. It took about four or five years for the restaurant to really have his imprint. His cooking is far less rich than my sort of cooking. Everything on the menu is extremely classic, still, but it has a lighter touch. He recognises the legacy, though. If he takes a dish out of the menu and puts on one of my favourites, he puts, 'in memory of my dad' underneath it. And if I have a party he will never fail to put one of those old dishes on for the evening. I was actually amazed when I went there for dinner to find those old favourites still there.

31. Cooking at home – with my faithful companions

So it is Michel's restaurant now, which makes me feel so proud. He has made it his own, but in a way that respects the place. That is how it should be. It's his style of cooking, and that what cooking is all about – style. If you make changes, hopefully you change them for the better, and in a direction that the client will appreciate. It is not a revolution but an evolution. And that is where I raise my hat to my son. I don't feel my jacket has been taken from me. On the contrary, meaning has been added to it. Of all the things I have achieved, he is certainly one of the most precious.

When I look at my life, I know I have been very lucky. I have worked hard, and I have enjoyed it, and I have had great rewards. At the end of the day, it comes down to doing what you love. You need to want to get up in the morning, and I always have. I have been up at 5 a.m. and happy to be so. With Le Gavroche, we set out to create a place for our customers to feel joy. I think we succeeded in that. And I have had joy too: in my career, in my family, and in the people I have known. That is what matters, in the end. As I said before, food is love. It is health and luck and life. And I have had more than my fair share of it all.

# ALBERT ROUX

## Three Appreciations

# Marc Beaujeu

———

*Chef and Executive Chef*
*at the Roux brothers' restaurants,*
*1969–2004*

Albert came into my life in 1969. I was in France, twenty-one years old, and I was looking for a job at a restaurant. I was a charcutier, but I wanted to cook, and that was difficult in France because every time I went for a job in a restaurant they would say, 'No, you are too old to cook now. Twenty-one is too late to learn.' At the time, the Roux brothers were opening Le Cochon Rose, their delicatessen in Lower Sloane Street, and they put an advert in a French newspaper looking for a charcutier with the possibility of doing some cooking. I found that advert and wrote to the brothers, and I got a letter back from Michel Roux saying they would be interested in offering me the job.

One month later, 1 June 1969, I was in London. I rang the office when I arrived, feeling a little bit lost because I came from the French countryside and here I was in the middle of London. 'Oh yes,' they said, 'we'll put you in a cab and send you to the staff housing on the Wandsworth Road.' When I arrived the door was opened by three girls who were living in the basement flat. 'There's no room here, it's full,' they said. 'We can't fit anybody else in.'

'So where will I go?' I said.

'Oh don't worry, we'll find something,' and eventually they found a sort of storeroom next to Michel and Albert's office which was used to store some dry goods. I slept there that first night, amid a strong smell of *herbes de Provence* and all sorts of produce. That was my introduction to it all. I came intending to stay for one year, and I lasted for thirty-five years in total.

When I arrived in England it was a bit of a shock, because living in France, good food was everywhere. Wherever you were, you could go to the shops and buy pâtés and foie gras and excellent charcuterie. But in England in the seventies? Not so much. The Gavroche was open Monday to Saturday, but on the Sunday when we were off, you couldn't find food anywhere. There were the Golden Eggs restaurants, where we could have eggs and bacon and pies. But delicatessens just didn't exist then. Perhaps if you could shop at Harrods, you could have found something, but for people like us there was nothing. The only bread was sliced in plastic packets, and in the pubs you could get a pickled egg from the jar. Now you have a bakery on every corner in London. For me it's the best place in the world to eat. You've got all the different foods, you've got shops everywhere, you've got people who are passionate and curious about food. The change in thirty or forty years is unbelievable. And so much of it is down to the Roux brothers.

Albert and Michel were fantastic. After about six months Albert came to see me to say I could start at the Gavroche. I began at the bottom – moving from station to station. Starters, vegetables, fish, I learned it all. We would do *dodine de canard* – duck deboned from the back – which was a complicated dish. You have to keep the meat and skin all together, stuff it with a foie gras stuffing and then sew it up. When we used to do that recipe, you could see the smile on Albert's face. It made him happy to cook food like that.

He was meticulous in his standards. If you did something and it was not right, he would put it in the bin straight away. 'Start again,' he'd say. The watercress soup, for example, had to be green like the green at Wimbledon at the start of the competition. If it was just a tiny bit yellow because it had been overcooked, you had to start again. You just could not serve it like that. Croutons would have to have a tiny bit of colour, but not too much. Every detail had to be perfect. He was a wonderful teacher to me; perhaps because I was a charcutier and his father had been a charcutier. We had a connection: he gave me attention, not just in cooking but in how to progress in my life.

Albert would take me to the markets often, because I had been involved with meat before so he knew I knew about it. We would finish work at 1 a.m. at the Gavroche and then at 5 a.m. there he would be, knocking on the door: 'Marc, time to go to the market.' On other days we used to play squash together in Dolphin Square, then have a sauna and rush to the Gavroche to start cooking. His energy was remarkable; he never stopped.

I stayed about a year at the Gavroche. One day I remember, we were short on washers up so Albert was doing the job. There he was in a T-shirt, a cigarette hanging out the corner of his mouth, doing the washing up, when the young guy the agency had sent us to help arrived in the kitchen. Of course, he had no idea who Albert was, so he said to Albert, 'Oh, are you washing up today?' and Albert replied, 'Oh yes, from time to time I do that job.' 'Well, is it hard work? What's the boss like?' And Albert just says, 'Oh, you know, it's OK.' So the guy is patting him on the back, asking him to show him the ropes, and then he said, 'Do you have a cigarette, because I don't have too much money.' So Albert gave him a cigarette. That guy certainly got a shock when he found out that Albert was the boss, but that was the kind of atmosphere there.

The brothers were still doing one week on and one week off at the Gavroche, which led to some interesting moments. It was the same at the Poulbot, where I went to work after the Gavroche. We cooked a lot of omelettes there – omelette after omelette, an unbelievable amount. When Albert was there, he said the omelette should be white, no colour on it at all. The following week it was Michel, and he liked it to brown a tiny little bit – you had to have a little colour on it. It was very confusing; you had to have your wits about you.

In 1975 I decided to go back to France, because I was finding it difficult to work in the City at that time – it was the era of the IRA, so there were blockades everywhere, you had to show that you were working in the restaurant to get through, all the letterboxes were closed off. It all felt too much. On top of that, one of those three girls who had welcomed me to the flat on that first night, Marlyse, had agreed to marry me and we wanted to return to France.

I went to see Albert and told him I wanted to go back. He said, 'OK, Marc, if that is your decision, I can't go against you.' But he was so clever, Albert. He used to know everything before you even told him. He said, 'Do you have something over there?' I told him that I had plans there to open up my own place. 'Well, Marc, it probably won't work, but you can always come back. Always. You will be most welcome.'

He came over to France for our wedding, and I started a restaurant in Saint-André-de-Corcy, between Lyons and Bourg-en-Bresse, in partnership with another chef. It was a one-star restaurant, and it was doing OK. But after a year I said to Marlyse, 'I just can't carry on living in France any more. I'm not happy, I'm not working enough, I don't like the atmosphere, I don't have enough to do.' I called Albert, who was in Lyons at the time, and the following day he came to see us. 'Marc, I don't know how to say anything to you. You remember when you left I said it probably won't work, but you know, it's only been a year. Take a bit more time, try to make a go of it.' So I stayed on, but after two years I called him again and told him I'd had enough – Albert said immediately, 'Well, no problem. If you want to come back then you have a job, Marlyse has a job, don't worry.' And that was it. I took my car, my dog, my knives, my hat and my apron. That was all we had.

Albert and Michel gave us a flat free of charge for a year because we had no money. He gave me the job of executive chef for the company, and Marlyse soon took up a position in 47 Park Street, the hotel above the new Gavroche. (The

32. Marc Beaujeu with Albert Roux

restaurant moved soon after we got back. They shut the Lower Sloane Street site on a Saturday night, and on the Monday opened up in Mayfair. Just like that.) The company was a big machine at the time. There was the Gavroche, the Waterside, Gavvers, the Poulbot, the Gamin, the outside catering. Hundreds of people working for them.

One day Albert came to me and said, 'I know what I'm going to do next; I'm going to open a butcher's shop.'

'Oh,' I said, 'that's probably a good idea.' Which it was, because London didn't have that kind of French boucherie at the time. 'But do you have someone who can run it?'

He said, 'Yes, I've got someone.'

'Who is that then?'

'It's you.'

I said, 'But I'm not a butcher, Chef.' And he answered, 'Yes, but you will be in a few months' time,' and sent me to Paris to do my training.

That was the start of Boucherie Lamartine. We opened up and it was immediately very successful. It was so busy. It led to us importing produce from France in a big way – Monique had stopped doing her journeys to Paris by then. We had first a van and then a bigger lorry and a truck, going once a week then twice a week. We would go to the Rungis market in Paris and pick up poultry, foie gras, everything. Then we started to bring in vegetables. Albert and I used to go to France often together, to find new suppliers. We'd travel all over the country. I'd say, 'Chef, I think I've found a new supplier for duck, let's go and meet them.' And off we would go. We met so many people and he used to charm them all. Eventually demand became so great that we had to open a place in Covent Garden. We made a huge success of selling to hotels and restaurants. Then Albert took over a poultry and game shop – near the Connaught hotel, and opened it up as Bailey's Lamartine to sell game.

That was Albert: he always had a new idea. I admit that sometimes I used to get fed up with him. He could be demanding, pushing you all the time. I'd say to him, 'Chef, you piss me off sometimes, you're going too far.' Or I'd have my own ideas, and say to him, 'Chef, I want a meeting with you next week.' And I'd come to his office with my own idea.

He'd say, 'How are you, Marco?'

I would say, 'Chef, I am fine, but I want to talk to you.'

'Talk to me, talk to me.'

So I would say, 'I think we should do this and this and this, and why are we doing this or that?' I used to come with my own ideas, and then of course I would leave the office with my head full of his ideas again. I'd laugh and say to myself, 'Marc, he's got you again.' He was a Napoleon, that guy.

People like Albert don't come into your life very often. If I hadn't written that letter, I would have a whole different life – my career, my wife, everything. When he disappeared, it was a disaster for me. He was family to me; he was my friend, but also my *père spirituel*, my father figure. He was such a big part of my life. He did so many things, he had so many ideas and helped so very many people, it was unbelievable. He had such a big heart.

# Silvano Giraldin

———

*Maître d' at the Gavroche,*
*1975–2008*

It still makes me laugh to think about my first encounter with Albert. I was a young man, twenty-two, and had applied to the Gavroche because I had tried the Connaught and the Savoy and got nowhere. Then a guy I knew suggested I try the Roux brothers – they were young and opening new places all the time so were employing a lot of people. I wrote to them, and ended up with a job as a waiter at the Gavroche. That was 1971.

When I arrived, the maître d' at the time, Angelo Poletti, pointed to a chair and said to me, 'Sit down there, Silvano, the owner will arrive in a moment to take you to the staff lodgings.' Everyone was very kind, offering me cups of coffee. I was all dressed up for my first day at work, in a jacket and tie, and I was a bit nervous. I didn't speak a word of English then, which was why I was glad it was a French company, because I had spent time in France and could speak the language. After a while sitting there, this guy arrived. He was a short stocky man, wearing a sort of white blouse thing over regular work clothes. It wasn't immaculately clean – he had obviously been moving meat around – and he had a fag in the corner of his mouth. He took one look at me and said, 'Let's go, I'll take you to your room.' And I said, 'No, no, I'm waiting for the boss to come.' To which he said, 'I am the boss. I'm the owner. Albert Roux.' Of course he had been at the markets, carrying a quarter of beef by himself so as not to have to pay the porter. That was typical Albert, to economise in that way. That was the very beginning of what was to be a long friendship.

At that time the two brothers were still doing turns of working in the kitchen, a week on, a week off. There were many differences between them. In cooking, Albert's food was probably more constant. Michel, being an artist, could be a bit more changeable, which is probably why the Gavroche got its three Michelin stars before the Waterside. And of course Albert was very much more the businessman. But Albert was not infallible in business. There were ventures which collapsed. What he always had were ideas – if he lost one business, it was on to two more. He was a real entrepreneur. Michel was perhaps better at the PR side of things and understood how to present what they were doing to the public. Albert couldn't care about that stuff. He was interested in cooking his food, creating his vision for the business. As for their relationship, they certainly loved each other – we knew not to get in between them – but that didn't stop them arguing. The best thing for us as staff was that we learned to play on it a little bit. If one of us was caught out doing something the wrong way, we realised we could say, 'Your brother told us to do that.' Even if it wasn't true, it would get us off the hook.

I became maître d' after a couple of years. I remember one night Albert came to me and said, 'You are short of staff tonight?', which was true. I said, 'Yes, I am missing a sommelier.' So Albert dressed himself up as a waiter with the black jacket and the bow tie and so on. At that time, we served the wine from a basket, and it was all going well, until a very beautiful lady arrived. Albert was serving another table at the time, and he completely lost concentration: he spilled red wine all over the back of one of the other female guests. The table's host jumped up and said to me, furious: 'Do you see what your waiter has done?'

'Don't worry,' I said, 'I'll send him home straight away.' Albert retreated to the kitchen, and at the end when the bill arrived, he wrote a note, saying, *I am the boss, sorry about that, the bill is on me. Please forgive me.* The table were very pleased in the end, and decided to come back the next day for another round.

In the beginning, the customers were unused to the kind of food we served. The brothers forbade things like smoked salmon, caviar, prawn cocktails, all the things that were popular in London restaurants at the time. We had a memo signed by both of them saying, *We will not serve well-cooked steak.* Because everybody wanted their steaks well done in those days. Sometimes we ended up trying to bribe the chef, saying, 'Come on, Chef, he's a good customer, can you not just cook his meat a little more?' Sometimes we did manage to get Michel or Albert to do it, but only under protest. Nowadays, we probably bend more to the customer: if the customer wants caviar, we give it to them. But of course that is not what they come to us for. At that time, people didn't know us. They took us for just another restaurant, and the thing was that the Roux brothers didn't want to be another restaurant, they wanted their own restaurant, to have their own identity. You can see that from their very first menu onwards. And it worked.

That generation was the springtime of French chefs. In France they invented nouvelle cuisine. Here, it was more what you would call new classic cuisine, and that was Albert and Michel. There was always a copy of Escoffier in the kitchen – they were always cooking with that in mind. They had self-belief, and they knew what they were doing. There was a big difference between the private house cooking they had been doing and restaurant cooking, but they became masters of it. They were clever also to surround themselves with a lot of people who knew about the business, and with good chefs who brought something that complemented their ideas.

There was no restaurant scene in London before Albert and Michel – they changed everything. The Gavroche was always the first to every accolade – to one Michelin star, two stars, three. They arrived at the right time and spotted the right opportunity, and if there was a barrier, Albert found ways to overcome it. Take the import–export side of the business, for example. You couldn't get the best goods in this country – everything was mass-produced – but Albert found a way to bring what we needed over here. Now if you go to the supermarket there are ten different types of eggs. You can see what a difference they made.

I lived round the corner from the old Gavroche site. What a difference from today – even as a young waiter earning very little money you could find yourself living in the best part of London. It was still a long day's work though – I would arrive at three in the afternoon, and last orders were at midnight. Six days a week. (Of all the restaurants, Gavroche was the only one that opened for six days, all the others were five, so we were always complaining about that.) The first thing would be to talk about the *Chef Propose* menu – Albert would have gone to the market in the morning and talked to the chefs about what to do with what he had picked up there. One strength of the Gavroche was that they always had marvellous chefs who could bring their own input, so they were taking part in what they were doing. It made them proud. But that was just on the *Chef Propose* menu. When it came to the main menu, there was a dictatorship. Although it was fixed by Michel and Albert, there would be a discussion with the chefs and myself when it came time to change it: this dish was a good proposition, this one was selling well, why don't we put this one back on?

People came back to the Gavroche time and time again. For Albert, that was the measure of success. In fact, we saw it tested later on, in 1989, when there was a brief scandal about the kitchen in the Gavroche being found to be dirty in an inspection. This wasn't true – the whole thing collapsed in court because there was no evidence at all. Albert knew it was rubbish and based on nothing. I remember him saying, 'You know, Silvano, I'm not worried, because the people who know us are still coming. From now on, if anyone cancels, forget them. Just remember the ones who are still going in the book.' And all our regulars did indeed come and support us so that financially we never suffered a moment. The restaurant remained full. We were on the crest of a wave. But Albert was very interested – as he said, now we can count our friends and see who they are. We had some regulars who are still regular now after fifty years. Sometimes their children are regulars too. I have not worked in Gavroche for twelve years now, and still whenever I go back there will be someone who recognises me, because they have been coming all that time.

We had all sorts of people at the Gavroche – the Queen Mother, Princess Diana, who would come in with Richard Attenborough. We had every movie star, as well as the powerful Hollywood players. The boss of Columbia pictures was a regular guest. Sam Spiegel came in. We had politicians and businessmen. Everybody. It was my job to make sure that they were all kept happy.

When the two brothers separated the business out, I became a director of Le Gavroche. It was nice for me, because around that time I had been headhunted to go and work at Claridges. I had a good offer from them in black and white. I showed it to Albert and told him he was paying me peanuts in comparison. Straight away he agreed to match it: 'The money is no problem, but wait a bit. Give me a couple of months.' Which I did, and then he offered me to be a director of the company. He promised always to look after me and sort me out, and he did. I have been looked after very well, with great generosity. That is what he was like. He was very loyal to his employees, and it wasn't just me – there were many others who

*33.* Silvano Giraldin

he helped in all sorts of ways. If somebody was in trouble, he would help them. Or if people wanted to start a new venture, he would support them, help them find the finance.

He had a large, generous nature. He was always giving you something. He was careful, but there was an extravagance of spirit. You could see it even in the way he approached the markets in the morning – he would always buy big. You'd ask him to get three sea bass, he would come back with ten or twenty. It was sometimes a nightmare for the chefs because he would find a good bargain and then say, 'You've got to use it all up.' Of course, it would make good financial sense, but it was also what he was like.

Albert was like a father to me. When you've been working for fifty years for the same people, they become family. He had a fantastic life. He made the most of it in every way, in business, in everything.

# Steven Doherty

——

*Head chef at Le Gavroche,*
*1985–1988*

I went to work at the Gavroche because I knew it was the best. I was at the Savoy at the time, but I realised that it wasn't going to do it for me. The big hotel restaurants in those days were like mirror images of each other – huge long menus, big brigades of chefs. I had drive, I had energy, and I wanted to work with the Roux brothers because they were the best in the business. At the Savoy, I tried to keep the fact that I was leaving a secret, but somebody obviously said something, because one of the boys came up to me and said, 'Oh, you're going to the Roux.' It was 1978, and the name was synonymous with quality.

I hadn't been in many kitchens by that point and had only worked in a couple of places. But I knew the Gavroche was going to be different from the outset. The Savoy must have had about a hundred chefs, at the Gavroche there were about six of us. I arrived just after the brothers stopped switching back and forth between the Waterside and the Gavroche, so I joined thinking Albert would be there. That was one of the main reasons I took the job. When I first turned up I was disappointed to find he was away – it was actually just for two or three weeks, but I didn't know that at the time. I thought, 'Oh lord, I've not walked into a job where the chef patron isn't actually in the kitchen, have I?' I spoke to Jean-Louis Taillebaud, who was the head chef at the time: 'Where's Mr Roux?' I asked. 'He's coming in a fortnight's time' was the answer. Thank God for that.

Even without Albert there, it was tough work. I knew it was going to be hard before I walked in the door. Jean-Louis was very good to me for those first two weeks. He really helped me along the way. But he did say to me, 'When Mr Roux comes back things will change.' And sure enough, when Albert turned up, he was like a whirlwind: this wasn't right, that wasn't right, why are you doing it that way? That was the start of it.

I had resolve, and it was a good thing I did. Those first four months were the hardest I've ever worked in all my career. It wasn't slave labour, but we were on a steep learning curve. I think Albert was on a mission at the time. He was pushing boundaries, pushing standards. We put new dishes on the menu, right across the board – desserts, main courses, starters. I got lucky, because my first station there was the pastry station and I'd been on pastry at the Savoy – I had enough training to get me going. I think if it hadn't been for that I wouldn't have made it. I was a petit commis then, not even a commis: a dogsbody at the bottom of the ladder.

Albert had the ability to spot talent very quickly in people – he always said he could turn a donkey into a racehorse.

The kitchen at the old Gavroche in Lower Sloane Street was certainly hot. People described it as a hellhole, but it wasn't really. It was a bit old, but it was functional. It worked well for what we were doing. I do remember though that when Rowley Leigh started, about a year after I did, he walked down the stairs, ruffled as always in this long grey army greatcoat. He walked into the kitchen, and right to the end of it where the skylight was. 'Where's the rest of it?' he asked.

'This is it,' I said.

'Where do you get changed?'

'In the room you just walked out of.' He couldn't believe that such food was coming from such a small space.

Albert Roux taught me to cook. After Jean-Louis left, René Bajard took over as head chef. He was a very good chef, and a good right-hand man who could translate what Albert wanted. When Albert was coming up with a new dish he would be hands-on, working one to one to show you how to cook it. Once it was perfect, it would be written up into the recipe files which contained every single dish that we ever did. It was all written down. He was a hard taskmaster: he might show you once, he might show you twice, after that you had to pick it up yourself. It wasn't that you were going to be in trouble, but you were going to get pushed a bit to make sure you got it.

Albert was determined. He was a very fair man and very generous. He knew exactly what he wanted and he could be a lunatic at service time, though I say that with fondness.

There was certainly some temperament on him, but he wasn't a bully in any way. In service time there was a lot of noise and shouting. It was theatrical, though, like Punch and Judy – there was no menace, no threat to it at all. Often it was actually funny, and some of the boys in the kitchen and I would be in the corner hiding because we were laughing our heads off. That was just the way it was. I remember a friend from outside the restaurant coming to see me once to drop something off. He was a bit late so service had already started, and one of the waiters came to fetch me. My friend was waiting up in the restaurant, and the intercom had been left on up there. All he could hear was Albert downstairs, shouting his head off. When I came upstairs, he was just open-mouthed: 'Who the hell is that, what's going on?' And I said, 'Oh, that's Albert.' He couldn't comprehend it. He told me later he thought they were animals. I just said, 'That's just the world we work in. They're not animals. We're not threatening each other, we're not going to kill each other, it's just the way it is.' It was all theatre, and it didn't detract from the incredibly high level of professionalism we were attaining.

Silvano wasn't afraid to let Albert have it, either. I remember Albert would be on the hotplate and at some point he would lose a check. Silvano would come in, screaming for the order. 'Where's table fourteen?' And Albert would look up at the checks on the tab grabber and say straight away, 'Oh yes! Fourteen! I'm sorry, Silvano, I missed it.' But he'd wait till Silvano had gone out the door and then fish it out of his pocket looking guilty. 'Kitchen, quick, quick, give me this! Give me that! I've made a mistake.' He'd put his hand up – he knew he was wrong. It was a regular occurrence because he was always stuffing the tickets into his pockets and forgetting.

In fact, in spite of the noise made, the team at the Gavroche was unusually tight, especially between front of house and the kitchen. The norm in those days was for the two to hate each other. I had seen that in action at the Savoy. But at the Gavroche it was different. In service time we'd have a go at each other because a check had come in wrong, or something had gone out to the wrong table – Silvano would come in all guns blazing, sometimes in Italian, sometimes in French. Then at the end of service, we'd have a glass of champagne, shake hands and it was never talked of again. We knew we were working together and were on the same side.

Albert worked like an absolute dog. He would go to the market in the morning, he would do lunch in the City at Le Poulbot or Le Gamin, and then he'd come to the Gavroche to do night-time service. Poulbot would be so busy at lunchtime, so to do a full service there and come back was really something. His drive was extraordinary.

As for his cooking – well, he was a genius. His food was generous and rich, which belonged not just to his own style but to the era in which we lived and cooked. In his obituary, Jay Rayner pointed out that Albert's cooking was very much of its time, and that was true. In those days, people wanted to leave a restaurant full. They weren't interested in looking at a couple of things on the plate. They wanted a good starter – scallops or langoustine or foie gras. And then main courses would be a prime ingredient: fillet of beef, fillet of veal, best end of lamb, slow-cooked dishes with sweetbreads. Fish would be turbot, Dover sole, lemon sole, langoustine or lobster. Cooking was probably easier than it is now: a big piece of protein, a garnish, a beautiful sauce. The customer was happy. People came to get fed: that was what was expected. If I do dishes for people now like that it just knocks them out – the sheer quality and flavours.

It was all very rich – we were using lots of cream, lots of butter in the sauces, heavy jus on the meats. We did a wonderful dish called a *tronçon* of turbot – you take a flatfish, split it down the bone, and then cut across, serve it with a red wine shallot sauce and spinach turnovers. It was a great dish. Or the sea bass *en papillotte*: you get a whole sea bass, gut it through the gills, then open it up through the back so there are no bones in it. Then you fill it with a creamy fennel mushroom filling, wrap it up in baking paper, bake it in the oven, and then cut the paper off, take the skin off, and serve it with golden butter on the top, breadcrumbs and hollandaise sauce and garnish. It's a glorious dish for two people. We'd do veal kidneys in a three-mustard sauce. Lobster with garlic butter. Lobster mousse with caviar and butter sauce. Or monkfish with a bourgignon garnish, button onions, bacon and mushrooms. It worked because the monkfish was so meaty. All these dishes were made using the best prime ingredients, and they were typically Albert dishes. At the time it was groundbreaking stuff. Now it's almost old school. So much of what we did then – the *tarte tatin*, the soufflé – everybody does it now, but that's where they came from. They are Roux signature dishes that have been copied to death.

I remember the lemon tart – the famous *tarte au citron*

that was invented when I first got there in September 1978. Albert had a recipe from his brother, but when I made it he got angry and said, 'That's not right, that's not right.' I told him I followed the recipe that he gave me. 'Yes, I know, but it's still not right.' So we served it that night, and then he came back to me the next day with the recipe slightly different. 'Right, let's do it again.' And it was perfect. That was it, that was the famous start of the lemon tart that the whole world makes now.

Some of the developments in cooking at that time came from the technology we could use. Non-stick pans transformed the way we cooked. Liquidisers transformed the way we cooked, the Robot Coupe, an early food processer, transformed things. Suddenly you could make light purees, light sauces, you could whisk things up at the end with the liquidiser. You could make mousses with the Robot Coupe, whereas when I was at the Savoy we were putting fish and shellfish and meat through a very fine mincer to get the meat fine enough. In the late 1970s and '80s fruit coulis were everywhere, because we had the liquidiser. Before that you'd have to cook it out – it would take for ever and you'd lose the structure of the sauce. Now you could cook up your raspberries and sugar and lemon juice, and with the liquidiser you'd have this glorious sauce in just ten minutes. I remember the first non-stick pans turning up in the Gavroche in late 1979. There was a salmon dish that the Troisgros restaurant made famous. When you look at it now, it seems like nothing – an escalop of salmon *à l'oseille*, salmon in a sorrel sauce – but it was revolutionary at the time. They made a very sharp fresh sauce with sorrel that had been blanched so that it stayed perfectly green. The sorrel went into the sauce at the last minute, and the salmon was cooked to order very quickly in the non-stick frying pan, which previously hadn't been possible, and then the salmon would go on the sauce on a plate. Boom. That was it – so simple, but the dish made the Troisgros' reputation. We did it at the Gavroche sometimes as a special. That was the kind of dish that was made possible by the new pans, and Albert took full advantage of it all.

I went to work for a short spell at Alain Chapel's in France in the early 1980s, and came back in 1982 to discuss what I might do afterwards. I remember Albert came up to me as I was having lunch and joined me, and said to me, very quietly, 'We've got our third Michelin star.' He was very calm about it but I knew what it meant, that it was massive. We celebrated with a glass of champagne. The media hadn't quite got wind of the news at that point, but when I went back to France there was a big story about Le Gavroche and the stars, how the brothers were the driving force behind the new movement of food in the UK. It was a big deal.

I became head chef in 1985. I was very fortunate to be given the position. I worked incredibly hard to get it, and I probably worked even harder when I was in charge. When I was being trained by Albert he used to say, 'When the food leaves that pass, that's it, it's gone. You've done what you've done. You're aiming for ten out of ten on every single dish you're sending. Nine is fine. Eight is OK. At seven, it's your call whether you send it out.' And those are the rules I used to work to when I became head chef. If something wasn't right on the pass, I wouldn't send it. I'd say to the boys, 'Right, that's not going out, you're going to do it again.' I remember once getting a real roasting from Albert – I got dragged into his office because I'd told off someone about something that wasn't right. 'You can't speak to people like that. And don't you dare say you picked it up from me!'

I was speechless. I wanted to say, 'Where the hell do you think I picked it up from?!' But I stopped myself. I said, 'Chef, it's like this. When you gave me the job, you had three stars. When I walk out of the building, you'll still have three stars.' He didn't say anything.

By then, we had pretty much every single accolade it was possible for a restaurant to have. We knew when the Michelin inspectors came back in: Silvano could smell them a mile off. It never worried us unduly because we knew that what we were serving day to day was of the standard that was expected.

Albert was a visionary. You could see that with the sous vide enterprise. He was fifteen years ahead of his time with that, at least. He set the business up, it didn't take off at the time, and it cost him a lot of money. It didn't have the impact that it should have with the wider public. It was very sad, really. But the number of chefs who came through the Gavroche kitchens and picked it up as a technique and used it was huge. In restaurants, it is everywhere now and has transformed cooking. He was just too early with it.

The way Albert cooked was on another level – it wasn't normal, it wasn't natural. He must have been born with the skill of being able to cook the way he did. When I first started cooking with him, I would sometimes just watch him, thinking, *How the hell did you learn this skill set?* He came from quite humble beginnings, and although he'd been trained by some good people, he wasn't trained by the great masters. His gift was just innate. When I first started at the Gavroche, I certainly wasn't a slacker, and I wanted to try and keep up with him. The speed the man could work was just extraordinary. His work ethic and productivity were unbelievable. I remember once he said to me, 'Ah, you can keep up with me now?' And I said, 'Yeah, just about, Chef.' 'Well,' he said, 'if you think I'm fast, you want to work with Pierre Koffmann.' Koffmann was known to be fast. But Albert was something else.

I would compare Albert to the great composers – Mozart, Beethoven, Brahms. There was something in there, something inside those people that made them what they were. And Albert had that gift, without a shadow of a doubt.

The connections that he had were just incredible, too. He knew everybody. People wanted to go to the Gavroche because they knew what it represented, and it represented Albert. When he got awarded the *Légion d'Honneur* by the French government, and there was a do at the Gavroche when he was presented with it by the French ambassador. I remember standing in the corner and looking around at the people who were in that room: powerful businessmen, industrialists, bankers, politicians. Everybody was there. That was a testament to the man that he was.

But in spite of all this, Albert was really humble. He knew what he was. There was this time when, through his connections, somebody asked him to find out something

34. Steven Doherty

about a business deal, something nobody could find out anything about. 'Leave it with me,' he said, and of course he soon found out what was going on. But how did he do that? People couldn't figure out how he got information it was deemed impossible to get. And he said to me, 'Ah, you know, people think I'm just a poor caterer.'

And I thought: *Enough said.* Of course, he was a caterer, at heart, but there was so much more to him.

# AFTERWORD

## *by*

# *Michel Roux Jr*

Life has always, always, been built around food for me. In that way I am like my father. My first memories are those moments when I sat under the big wooden central table in the kitchen at Fairlawne, playing with the lump of spare dough my father had given me. And then, in the same kitchen, a clear recollection from very early on of 'helping' Dad make vanilla ice-cream. I don't know how early you can have memories from, but I know I was very young indeed when I first turned the handle of the ice cream machine. It wasn't even really a machine – it was an old-fashioned pail with crushed ice and salt lining the internal cylinder. Dad would pour in the mixture and I would turn the handle, which moved the paddles through a crankshaft. You would hear the ice crack and crackle as the salt hit it. The anticipation of turning that handle! At the time it felt like forever, though I know now it would have taken about twenty minutes. And the final moment – I had seen my dad pour that liquid in, and then, hey presto, he opened it up and this beautiful creamy frozen texture came out. It was sheer magic.

Ever since I was a tiny child, a baby even, everything revolved around the table, and just the enjoyment of meals in general. Not in a fancy or chichi or expensive sense, just an appreciation for what we had. It was everything from pulling the carrots out of the ground and eating them, to going fishing and sitting down later to eat the fish. Or just collecting snails together, as we did in Kent – Mum and Dad would take us out as soon as it had finished raining to gather them. At Fairlawne I would sometimes be looked after by Mrs Bradbrooke, the wife of the chief butler there. She would make amazing puddings: baked apples, steamed puddings, crumbles topped with Bird's custard. Lovely. All my early memories seem tangled up in the pleasures of eating.

For all of that, I had Dad to thank. But not just Dad. Food memories for me come from every member of the family. My mother is a wonderful cook, and my grandmother was too – I remember well those walks with her at Fairlawne, foraging for strawberries or cress or whatever was in season. The whole family shared the same passion – my uncles, my aunties, the three grandparents I knew. Everyone had food at the heart of their lives, even the ones who didn't make a living out of it. My Uncle Jean, for example, on my mother's side – he wasn't a chef, he was an insurance broker, but food to him was the most important thing. He would think nothing of travelling the whole way across Paris just to get a Camembert because that was the best place to get them, and then taking an hour-long trip to the other side of the city to find some lamb chops at the best butcher he knew. Food was of huge importance. It wasn't about anything extravagant – not caviar or smoked salmon – but getting the best ingredients that you could afford, and then celebrating them by cooking them in the best possible way.

Our home in Shipbourne – the Pink Cottage – was testament to this family passion. There was the garden where my father would plant loads of vegetables, the kitchen where my mother (usually) would cook for us. In my memory our little cottage wasn't little at all, it was huge – a great big lawn out front and a massive kitchen garden and a shed out the back. But I have visited it as an adult, and it is in fact tiny – a lovely little cottage with a small lawn out front. It all felt enormous to me back then; it was my whole world.

~

Reading my father's memories in this book has been bittersweet. How lovely to be reminded of some of my best childhood memories. Those summers in Shipbourne when the extended French family would come over, bringing with them all kinds of treasure – Camembert, salamis, cured meats, chocolates. There would be wonderful get-togethers in the garden in summertime or inside in winter. The place would be full of laughter and joy; it was all huge fun and merriment with lots of food and wine, and every adult smoking because everybody smoked back then.

In particular, my Uncle Michel would come. He was a

joyous presence in those days, and he lit up something in my father as well – they would be jumping up and down with laughter, slapping each other's backs and joking. Just having huge fun together. I remember him doing his sugar work in the Fairlawne kitchens. It was astounding to a child's eyes – it seemed he could make anything: beautiful flowers and fruit and fantastical creations. The kitchen would be filled with the smell of the caramel, and the sound it makes as you work it: a cracking sound as you pull the sugar. It was like having a sorcerer in the family.

That relationship changed when Dad and Uncle became business partners. The family get-togethers still happened, but there was something more serious in their relationship, because they were working together and they didn't see eye to eye on everything. What you can read in the book – the constant push and pull of their relationship – is part of what made Le Gavroche great. My uncle the artist, the details man, fastidious in his cooking and his approach to work. My father perhaps more attacking in his approach, both to cooking and life.

I have quite often been asked whether, if they were both to cook the same recipes, there would be a difference between the resulting plates, and the answer is yes, I would be able to tell who had cooked what. Neither would be better, but there would be a difference. My father's cooking was perhaps more robust in depth of flavour, whereas my uncle's was more refined, subtle and precise. Uncle was tremendously creative – his pâtisserie and sugar work were testimony to this. The savoury side was secondary, though of course extremely skilled. Dad was very much savoury. His forte was sauces, and also charcuterie, pâtés and terrines. Things where you needed to roll up your sleeves and get going. Perhaps it was partly because, being that much older, Dad was the one who as a child spent more time living above the charcuterie. Who knows? Certainly his cooking was gutsy and had enormous depth. Their personalities were there on the plate, and they were two totally different characters. But both passionate about the end result.

It was the same in business. My uncle was very careful and frugal and a little risk averse. My father was a gambler, an entrepreneur who loved risk. Again that was perhaps the reason they were so successful. They bounced off each other, but they both had the same goal, which was perfection. It was all about the pursuit of excellence. They were both heading for the same place, but with a different route, stylistically speaking.

It is often described as a love-hate relationship – and it definitely was that too – I've seen them argue till they were red in the face and swearing at each other, and then within seconds they were hugging and kissing. They were not afraid of picking up on the other's weaknesses. They genuinely did have a massive brotherly love, a very strong bond, but put them together in a room and in ten minutes they might be at each other's throats.

$\sim$

Of course, for the family everything changed when they opened Le Gavroche. We went from living in this lovely pink cottage in Shipbourne with Dad around all the time, to a house in the London suburbs. Our new house had a garden, but it could hardly rival the countryside and the grandeur of Fairlawne. There were busy streets, and we were suddenly taking the bus everywhere. Even the smell of London seemed strange after the countryside. School was different – the food at home was somehow different, though still terrific, since my mum was cooking every day and she is a great cook. But for my mother, myself and my sister Danielle, the biggest change of all was family life, because suddenly we no longer really saw Dad. He was working all hours – understandably so. He would come back on a Sunday exhausted and then sleep all day to recharge for the week ahead before he went back to work on a Monday. The hospitality industry can be brutal for this, let alone when you are breaking new ground as my father and uncle were.

Reading his account of this time, I am struck again by what a brave and radical move that change was. He truly loved the Cazalets and his life there, and it must have been a wrench for him as well as us. It is hard not to read his recollections as a love letter to that family: he never forgot his gratitude to them. And rightly so, because without them there would not have been Le Gavroche. Maybe another backer would have come forward eventually, but it would have taken years longer to establish. Going from private service to running a restaurant was a huge leap for both the brothers, neither of whom had ever worked in a restaurant setting before.

But Dad was always extremely ambitious – right up until the end he had a restlessness to do the next thing. So for all the delights of Fairlawne, I think there was just a burning need to make the most of the opportunity he could so plainly see. His business mind must have been working overtime – he knew there were very few restaurants of any note in the UK, and he knew he could do it brilliantly. It must have been difficult to weigh up against the lovely life he had built, but there was always that drive inside him – I think he just had to do it.

While food and cooking simply ran through Dad's veins, he was also a businessman. About business, he was passionate, and more than willing to take a gamble, as his many enterprises show. He loved risk and thrived on it – perhaps unsurprisingly, he was a very good poker player too. But it would always be a considered risk. He was extremely good at working out odds and he would make sure that everything was stacked up and ready and the chances of failure were minimal. It would have been Dad who wanted to get several restaurants up and running as quickly as possible, whereas my uncle was more reserved and slower, wanting to go step by step. You can see that again later in the way he took the gamble of moving his very successful restaurant from Lower Sloane Street to Mayfair: he was throwing the dice, but in a way he had considered carefully. And it paid off.

Dad was always particular about doing things by the book. He wanted his businesses to be run in the proper manner, as though they were FTSE 100 companies. Even the smallest of them would have the full treatment: AGMs, a chairman, a secretary, a board of directors. It can be quite amusing to read the minutes – my uncle, my father and another director, carefully minuting that the food cost is 1 per cent out, or that the washing-up liquid supplies are being bought from the wrong place, before earnestly discussing how to do it better. But that was Dad. Things had to be run in a certain way.

He knew, as any successful restaurateur must, that the line between success and failure lay in the detail of the accounts. But although he was always meticulous about costings and very careful with commodities, sometimes he would just go wild and create a dish that would be brilliantly over the top. That was his generosity and extravagance coming out. Or he would spot a bargain at the markets and be unable to resist, driving the chefs mad by suddenly coming back with ten trays of apricots which they then had to figure out how to use, because there was nothing he hated more than waste. He abhorred it. As far as he was concerned, nothing should ever go in the bin.

He was clever, too, at surrounding himself with brilliant people. That's something he always insisted on – if something's not your skill set, if you don't understand it, or it's not your job, get someone in to do it, and trust them to get on with it. Otherwise, don't employ them. It's a mindset he instilled in me too, and that I now say to up-and-coming chefs: play to your strengths. If you're not expert in a particular field, get professional advice.

It's astounding that with the opening of the Gavroche, my father and uncle launched not just their own successful restaurant, but a revolution in how people cook and eat in this country. I look at the first menu from the Gavroche now and within it I can see the bones of the brothers' origins, and, already, everything Le Gavroche stood for. French, traditional, classic. There is a strong sense of their shared cooking history: the dishes are variations of what they would have served in private houses. It is very much of its day – the *selle de veau Orloff*, the poached chicken and Armagnac sauce. Those are diehard classics, and yet, variations of many of the first dishes still appear on our menu from time to time now – the watercress soup, or the *Soufflé Suissesse.*

Take the *pot au feu sauce Albert*. That is a dish that is very much my father, and not just in name. A staple of French country cooking, but elevated due to the excellence of his technique. It's a dish you can't mess around with too much. The beauty of it lies in the precision of the cooking rather than the presentation. That was Dad's forte: he was all about robust cooking, and you can't get much more robust than a *pot au feu* – after all, at heart it is boiled meats. But in Dad's hands it wasn't just any old plate of boiled meats. Everything was simmered at the right temperature and cooked to perfection. Tender and flavourful. You can't make the *pot au feu* look that elegant: it is a plateful of goodness, and that is what it looks like – hearty. It's the same thing with the *soufflé suissesse*. We have it on the menu still, and occasionally get comments from people saying that the presentation isn't grand and perfect. Well, it's a soufflé that's cooked on a bowl of cream, and I'm afraid that is just what it looks like. Nothing will embellish it, but it is wonderful to eat. It is about making sure that you have perfect ingredients cooked with precision. My father used to say that even scrambled eggs could be three-star Michelin scrambled eggs. And of course they can be. Indeed, at the Waterside my uncle had a dish called *oeufs brouillés aux oeufs* – scrambled eggs with eggs. It was just a celebration of eggs: perfect scrambled hen eggs, poached pigeon eggs, salmon eggs and caviar. A simple dish, elevated.

With both my father and my uncle, that was the goal: to take the best ingredients and celebrate them. It wasn't about the garnish or the furbelows. I've dined on several occasions with Dad in places with a very modern fussy approach, and it was never to his liking. The fewer tweezers and froths and foams applied to food the better, in his opinion. Overworked food used to really put him off. In particular he had a hatred of edible flowers and the overuse of herbs on a plate. If something like that landed in front of him, the first thing he would do would be to religiously pick off all the flowers and all the herbs. It had probably taken the chef maybe five minutes to dress that plate, and he would ceremoniously and methodically pick them all off – not just pick them but throw them, and then get to what he was actually interested in, which was tasting the food.

I suspect it used to send a bit of a shiver down peoples' spines when the old man used to walk into a restaurant. I remember a moment a few years ago when I invited Dad for a Sunday lunch with his wife Maria and my daughter Emily and her husband Diego. He and I used to like to wind each other up a bit, so without telling him I booked an Indian restaurant. 'You did this?' he said as he arrived, because he was never a fan of curry.

'Yes, I booked it, great place,' I said.

'But it smells of curry in here.'

'Yes, it's an Indian restaurant,' I replied, just as the manager arrived at the table to take the order. He obviously recognised Dad, but he handled it beautifully when Dad looked at him, completely straight-faced, and said, 'I hate curry.'

'Don't worry, Mr Roux, I'm sure we can find something for you to eat,' he said. Which they did – they grilled some prawns for him which were marinated in something delicious and quite mild, and he thoroughly enjoyed it with some perfectly steamed rice. As he left, he called the manager over with a huge smile on his face. 'You were right,' he said, 'that was bloody good.'

It was a joy to him to discover something delicious.

～

For myself, it was always obvious to me that I would work in kitchens. There was nothing else that I wanted to do. Although I enjoyed sport, nothing else at the various schools I went to attracted me at all. School just wasn't for me. There was one thing I had in mind and that was to work. To earn a living. Perhaps more than anything else that was what my dad instilled in me. You have to do something in life: you can't just sit on your backside and expect to be looked after. You don't stay idle.

It wasn't necessarily that I wanted to have my own restaurant or follow in my father's footsteps to be a chef. I just wanted to be in a kitchen – I loved the camaraderie, the atmosphere, the smell. Even as a child I could see that kitchens were a place where magic happened, and I wanted to be part of that.

It was probably Mum as much as Dad who taught me to cook. I watched her make classic French dishes like *pot au feu* or boiled tongue. I started just by being in the kitchen observing how it was done, and then I began helping her make sauces, vinaigrettes – the basic stuff. I would do it alongside her, or my sister and I would help as she made Sunday lunch or when family or guests were around. We would be roped in as assistants, and then sit down to eat with everyone. That was very important – there was no 'adults eat here, children over there'; children were always part of the meal, and we did not leave the table till we were told to.

My first job, as a young teenager even before I left school, was washing the dishes and the pots and pans at Le Poulbot. It was during the summer holidays, and I filled in for the kitchen porter there – a lovely guy, originally from Senegal I think, called Nestor. He showed me the ropes on the first couple of shifts and then I was on my own. The chef, Chris, took absolutely no prisoners. 'You're filling in for him, you've got to do his job properly.' And it was a tough job, but I loved being part of the team. As a KP, your work is important. Chefs need clean pans, and they must be pristine and ready the moment they are required. They need spuds for the chips, which as KP you have to peel. The kitchen must always be spotless. You can't let the rest of the team down. It was all a responsibility, and I craved responsibility. Not to mention the fact that I was being paid – I bought my first bike, a Great

British Holdsworth, through that job, and a stereo set and lots of things.

I certainly wasn't treated with kid gloves because of who my dad was. And definitely not by him. When my father or my uncle were in the kitchen there was absolutely no quarter given, no favours. On the contrary, it was 'Move your arse, get on with it!' But I loved it.

Seeing Dad working the pass at the Gavroche was quite something. The theatricality of it, bellowing the orders out and waiting to hear back – 'Oui, Chef!' 'Yes, Chef!' It was all very old school, but that was very much Dad and the way he ran the pass and the kitchen. If I'm really honest it wasn't extremely well organised, but it worked for him. There was certainly always some dramatic shouting in Dad's kitchens. And kitchens in that era could be tough places to work. But Dad wouldn't tolerate any kind of bullying atmosphere. There was no physicality, and no meanness.

In the early days he was very hands-on: he'd roll up his sleeves and get mucky, really work a section. Later in life it was more about the chefs bringing him the plates of food and him appraising them. But nothing was getting past him: if he saw anything that was remotely wrong or not the way he would like it done he would pick up on it immediately. There was no way anything substandard was going out into the restaurant.

He kept a beady eye on everything: and that meant how people were working as well as the food they were preparing. Being a great chef isn't just about the end product, the plate of food. It's also about how you get there. Obviously you need the best ingredients, and you need to know where they come from. But it's also about how you treat those ingredients, all the way through. Take something as simple as picking up a steak. How are you going to hold it, and how are you going to cook it? You need to treat it with respect; you don't just throw it on the grill. When anyone did that, Dad didn't like it at all – and quite rightly. Even with a dirty pan, you don't just hurl it in the sink. You remove the excess fat, if there's anything burnt in it you scrape it down, and then you place it in the sink – you don't dump it – and you tell the washer-up that it's hot. There should be respect in *everything* you do. And there should be communication. I learnt all of that from my dad.

As a boss, as a mentor, as a teacher, my father was quite a presence. He wasn't tall, but he was an imposing character. You knew when he had walked into the room. He was physically a very strong man, and mentally he was strong as well. If he looked you in the eyes and said something, well, you didn't question it. He could be a tough boss, with me as much as anyone, but he was driven by his desire to get the best out of everybody. From cleaners all the way up, he wanted to push each individual – not just for the good of the company but for the good of the person.

He could be hard to work with or work for, but there was never any malice or meanness. If things didn't work, they didn't work. He would give you several chances. He might even give you a dressing down or two. Then, if he felt standards were still not being met, he would say, 'OK, goodbye, this isn't working.' But that goodbye didn't mean he wanted to forget about you. It was more a case of: 'Goodbye, but don't forget to let me know where you are, because if I can ever help you in the future I will.' And many times he did: if people weren't a good match for the Gavroche he might direct them somewhere that he thought would suit them better. There was always care there, because he had a generosity of spirit that ran through everything he did.

There's no doubt he was inspiring. It wasn't just that he passed on his vast knowledge about cooking, it was his whole approach to life and to work. He venerated hard work, professionalism and craftsmanship. When it came to the food, technique mattered – and he passed that on to those he worked with.

Above all, the importance of provenance was highlighted. Sometimes, when I was young, Dad would say, 'Do you want to come with me to the market tomorrow?' This was the signal for a great adventure. Waking up early was hard, but then we would be careering through the dark streets of London in Dad's van, stopping first at the old fish market in Billingsgate. It was a whirlwind – the smell of the place, the noise, the shouting of the porters, the rattle of the carts on the cobbles: those old carts didn't have tyres, they had old wooden and iron wheels. The porters would be carting them around at high speed, and they wouldn't stop: they would just shout for you to get out of the way and God help you if you didn't. They wore hats with flat tops so they could stack the crates on their heads. It was a different world, and one with almost its own language – old pounds, old weights, old measures. There would be huge drawers of fresh eels, which I found fascinating, along with every other kind of fish you could imagine.

Dad was in his absolute element in the markets, charging through the hubbub. He kept his money in a big leather satchel, his cash at the ready so he could quickly get the produce in the van and set off to the next market. We'd be weaving through the streets in the little van at a hundred miles an hour till we hit central London, where it would be gridlocked. Dad would hurl the van to a stop – double, triple-parked, it didn't matter. And then he'd have catapulted out of the van and shot off at top speed through the meat market. My biggest fear was losing him, so I would be tailing him as fast as I could. He'd be going double time, grabbing this, assessing that. He would hoist a side of beef on his back, to the fury of the porters who would chase him down the alleys shouting, 'You can't effing do that!' – he'd just shrug and talk back to them in French, usually with a fag hanging out the side of his mouth. He'd chuck the beef into the van and off we'd head to Covent Garden. It was an onslaught for all the senses. Introducing me to the market life was his way of indoctrinating me in all the work that goes into a restaurant – and I loved it.

When I was around fifteen, Dad and I were on a fishing trip together in Ireland. He loved fishing: it was like a religion for him. I took the opportunity to talk about the future with him. 'Listen, Dad,' I said, 'I really don't want to go into further education. I want to leave school once I'm sixteen, and I want to be a chef.' As he put it later, he almost jumped into the sea with joy. He hadn't pushed me into the choice, but there is no doubt he was over the moon. He gave me a big hug, and then we caught a sea bass and spent a good long while discussing how to cook it. I remember him saying, 'Leave it to me, we'll try and work out the best place for you to do an apprenticeship.'

A short time later he came back to me and suggested that I do a pastry apprenticeship in Paris, as he had. I think he probably consulted my uncle, who being the *pâtissier* would have known the very best places to go. Not long later I was leaving to do my two years apprenticeship at Hellegoarche, the famous and wonderful *pâtisserie* in Paris. My father's advice as I set off was straight and to the point: 'Don't mess it up like me, son.' He had loved his apprenticeship, but he knew it was going to be very hard work, and I think he was hoping I wouldn't get in trouble for naughtiness as he had.

So there I was at sixteen, in Paris and in many ways following my father's footsteps. I stayed with my grandmother in the tiny family flat in St Mandé, sleeping on the sofa as he probably had. My grandmother was still polishing those floors to a high shine, and the kitchen in that little place was full of the jams and preserves that she made in the season, still very much the French countrywoman. Every afternoon she would sit down to tea – a hangover from her time in England. She loved to slurp her tea, but whenever my father heard her do it, he would give her an earful. She would protest, 'But Mrs Cazalet always used to slurp . . .' She would also have a treat which I think was particular to her: she would drop a lump of stale bread into one of those French Pyrex glasses – there would always be stale bread around because she would never throw anything away – and then she would add a sugar lump and a splash of red wine to make a kind of purple paste. It was her pick-me-up for the afternoon.

I would have a weekly call from Dad. He would ask if it was tough and I would tell him, 'Of course, but I'm loving it.' Which was true. Much of what I was doing on that job would have been similar to what my father had done all those years before. He knew how hard the work could be, but he also knew how much I would learn.

That apprenticeship was followed by my French military service, which I served in the Élysées Palace. At that time, you got a place there by pulling strings, and Dad and Uncle did so for me. It was a bit complicated, because there were elections at the time, and when a new president comes in they sometimes have a cleanout of the staff at the Élysées, so it looked like the people who my father and uncle had spoken to to get me in might have been out of a job. But it worked out all right. Giscard D'Estaing was out and Mitterrand was in, but the chains were not broken and I was fortunate to get the job. I did two months proper military training and then I was moved to the palace where I was cooking first for D'Estaing and then for Mitterrand. Weirdly, a letter was sent to all of us saying that they would understand if we wanted to move on because of our political allegiance, though I'm pretty sure nobody did. You'd have been mad to.

My military service was very different from my father's. Here I was in the centre of Paris, cooking in the grandest of kitchens, while he had spent his dodging bullets in Algeria. But I did know that he had cooked in these kitchens himself, seconded there from time to time when he was at the British embassy down the road. It was a strange echo from the past.

After my military service ended, I worked for a time at Alain

Chapel's restaurant in Mionnay. I remember at that time Mum and Dad coming out to see me for my twenty-first birthday. We had an epic lunch (of course) at Paul Bocuse in Lyons, enjoying each other's company and the marvellous food. We were all so full and happy afterwards that we collapsed on a lawn in the sun next to the banks of the Rhône and had a siesta. It was a perfect afternoon.

My next move was to the Mandarin Oriental in Hong Kong, and then back to London to work at La Tante Claire under Pierre Koffmann. After that, I worked in Le Poulbot, as well as Gavvers, and the outside catering division.

I was working at Le Gamin when the pastry chef at Le Gavroche went on holiday. My dad called and said, 'Come to the Gavroche, help us out, because we need a pastry chef for a couple of weeks.' So I did. And then the sous chef went on holiday and I filled in for him, and before I knew it, I found myself staying on. My father at that time was still the executive chef, with Steven Doherty as the head chef, and it must have been around then that Dad started to think about moving on from being in charge.

∽

If I stand back from my dad as a father, and think of him as a chef, I share the opinion of everyone else: together, my father and uncle changed the culinary geography of this country. They arrived here when food was typically brown, dull and uninspiring. By the end of their lives, three-star Michelin restaurants were flourishing up and down the country, and good food, good ingredients and good cooking had become part of the national conversation. It's not an exaggeration to say that a huge part of that change was due to them: the restaurants they opened, the chefs they trained, the customers they fed, the books and TV they created. In the industry, they are looked on as pioneers, and rightly so. They were inspirational. They inspired some people to come into the industry, making it look important, interesting and valuable. For others, it was just the inspiration to care about food: to cook and to be curious and passionate about what we eat and to ask questions.

Their seismic effect on the restaurant industry wasn't just about influencing chefs. They revolutionised front-of-house service, and they also had a huge impact on the suppliers. It became a trickle-down thing: more and more chefs were getting trained in the Roux way, and they in turn demanded more and more good produce. So the more chefs were trained, the more they asked the growers to farm in different ways. And that in turn led to customers who were more and more discerning and knowledgeable, and thus to further demand for the best. They both believed that knowledge is key, and they were passionate about passing it on.

And pass it on they did. The list of distinguished chefs who passed through the various Roux kitchens is famously long – Pierre Koffmann, Marco Pierre White, Gordon Ramsay, Rowley Leigh, Marcus Wareing, Bryn Williams, Monica Galetti, my cousin Alain Roux . . . it goes on. On top of that there are 'second generation' Roux influences: the chefs who worked under the brothers in the seventies or eighties who have gone on to train another ream of chefs, who are now training up another load. You could draw it like a family tree, and see the branches of influence stretch out to encompass a huge swathe of the British restaurant industry. The tendrils of their influence are everywhere.

I believe that if you walk into a restaurant that carries the Roux philosophy at its heart you can spot it straight away. No matter what the food is, the bones of what make a Roux-influenced restaurant are discernible under the surface. First, a care for ingredients and a solid founding in technique. Classic French technique, visible in the rudimentaries like a good sauce. But beyond this, the word that springs to mind is generosity. Generosity is very much a Roux trait – not just in the size of portions (which is important), but generosity in taste and in hospitality. The service will be not cold and aloof but warm, open and friendly. At Le Gavroche this is something instilled in me and in the fabric of the place: make sure the diners are coming to somewhere that feels like a private house. We're in the hospitality industry and it needs to feel hospitable. That sense of conviviality comes directly from my father. The desire to be there, on the restaurant floor, actually greeting guests and making sure they feel welcome. That was the whole raison d'être of Le Gavroche. It was part of his vision.

Then there will be generosity behind the scenes – is the chef or the restaurant generous in its time, in its teaching? That is very much a Roux trait, and again, part of my father's character. Those are the building blocks – things which are in some ways intangible. You might not be able to put your finger on it, but you know it's there, right from the moment you walk into the restaurant. That feeling of at-homeness starts, as far as the customer is concerned, with the front-of-house staff, and here my father and uncle were revolutionary.

There is an old French saying in the restaurant trade: '*On ne melange pas le torchon et la serviette*' – don't mix the dishcloths with the napkins. The two don't gel. When my dad came into the restaurant trade, front of house were considered a different breed. He was always trying to break that wall. The practice at Le Gavroche, for example, was that chef apprentices should do a couple of months in the room. They used to take the kitchen and front-of-house teams off together to do what would now be called team bonding – football or bowling or staff parties. Whether or not this was a conscious decision to make the staff get on with each other, I am not sure, but I do know that that barrier has been broken down enormously in the industry and that was very much a Roux thing.

This is not to say that Dad didn't used to have flaming rows with the front-of-house staff. I can see him and Silvano at it now – absolutely furious, poking each other in the chest, storming off in different directions. And with Tony Batistella the manager too. As the very first person who was employed at the Gavroche, he and Dad had a strong bond. Both had come to the UK as young men from rural backgrounds on the continent. Both had been born just before the war and known the feeling of wartime scarcity in post-war Europe. They fell out time and again; Tony had his way of working and my dad had his. But at the end of service they would sit down and have a glass of champagne together, all forgiven.

It was the heat of the moment, and forgotten as soon as it was done. Tony was part of the family, and such a warm and generous man. Underneath the noise and bluster, they loved each other, and had friendships that lasted right till the end. Tony sadly died just before Dad did, something that upset him very much.

~

If you look back at the whole arc of Dad's life, there is so much to be proud of. The legendary restaurants he founded. The businesses he developed. The seismic influence he had on the food industry. The countless awards and accolades he had from the industry and beyond – lifetime achievement awards, the Cateys, the *Légion d'Honneur*, the Papal Knighthood and the OBE. The OBE, in particular, meant something really special to him because he was, till the end of his days, so passionate about this country.

Then of course there were the Gavroche's groundbreaking three Michelin stars, the first in the country. They cemented its status as a landmark restaurant. It is hard to know exactly how my father felt about the Michelin stars. He always said he cooked for the customer, not for the Michelin Guide, and of course he was right. What he impressed on me is that you should cook in your own style, doing what's right for you and your customers. Don't cook for the Guide, don't cook for the plaudits. Do what you think is right, make sure your guests are happy, because that's number one. If they are happy they will come back, then the accolades will follow. But don't get it the wrong way round. Deep down, though, I'm sure he cared a lot about the stars: it's an achievement to be very proud of, one where you become part of a very small elite group of chefs. You have to work very hard to get them, and there is no doubt that he did. But if he had to choose between three stars or a full restaurant of happy guests? I'm sure he'd say, 'Get rid of the bloody stars, give me the happy guests every day of the week.'

Above all, I think what he might have been most proud in his life was having trained so many people and made the industry what it is today. He would get letters and emails from all over the world from people who had worked under him and who were now setting up their own places. Nothing gave him greater pleasure. He was constantly striving to improve every corner of our trade. There is still plenty to do, but his influence has made huge changes for the better.

～

Moving on from Le Gavroche must have been a tough decision for my father. Certainly, the years after I took over were interesting ones for us. I don't think I was quite mentally prepared for the challenge, and Dad wasn't really prepared to let go either. He would tell a different story, but even when he said he was retiring from Le Gavroche, he was still there! I couldn't get him out of the place. He certainly didn't sign a piece of paper and disappear into the sunset. But it's understandable. He had built Le Gavroche from nothing: it was his creation. Both sides certainly had their challenges;

letting go for him must have been just as difficult as taking it on was for me. He could be a tough critic. And there were a lot of challenges for the restaurant at that time; in terms of customers, we were busy as hell, but financially things were not straightforward. I was working crazy hours, and there was no doubt a huge stress from the responsibility of taking over and keeping everything afloat.

I think the decision to step back from his role as executive chef was the right one for him. It was never about retiring. Dad was always going to work. But he had so much more that he wanted to do, opportunities he wanted to follow up. Because, to go full circle, he knew that while he was in charge of Le Gavroche it was important that he should be here. The boss, the owner of the place should be around, to meet and greet and be hospitable. And that was a tie. Passing the apron across to me, as he put it, meant that he could chase up different challenges: consultancies with Marks and Spencer and British Airways, interests in hotels as far flung as Geneva, Amsterdam and America. He was still consulting for the Compass Group and others, and opened up the successful Chez Roux restaurants in Scotland. He carried on working at full pelt.

He remained a director of Le Gavroche, and he certainly believed in being hands-on. He would ring up the chefs once a week: 'How are you doing? What's the price of sole? How much are you paying for this or that?' He loved all that. He would read all the accounts, in forensic detail. He loved analysing figures, and he remained needle-sharp about it right to the end.

For his other restaurants, the chefs and managers would be sending down a weekly report, which his secretary Anne-Marie would print out for him because there was no way he was reading on a computer or phone. He'd work his way through this big pile of reports, diligently answering them where need be. There were the menus to go through and pass comment. Then there was the travel to all the various places where he had interests, especially in the early days. Even right towards the end he was going up to Scotland every six to eight weeks to visit the restaurants up there. He always loved Scotland – drawn to the wildness, the country air, the produce. He loved the Scottish people and their attitude to life and was very proud of training a lot of Scottish chefs and showcasing them. He worked with different colleges there and was involved with an initiative called Adopt a School where he would go into primary schools and do taste tests with the children. He loved doing that.

Then there were the annual events that he consulted on for the Compass Group: Wimbledon, Epsom, Newmarket – all sorts of high-profile occasions. This was not just a question of signing off on the odd menu, he was involved in every stage. For a large event like Wimbledon or Epsom – which he was doing right up until lockdown came – he and I would team up with the executive chefs around eight or nine months in advance to go through the previous year's menus, work out what had worked, what could be improved on, and what we wanted to do this year. We would then propose the menu and wait for the client to come back and express their preferences – more vegetarian options, say, or different choices for desserts. Once we had refined the menus we would work towards a date, the actual tastings, when the executive chefs and their teams would get everything ready. Right up until lockdown put an end to it, he would be there at the tastings, where we would go through the menus dish by dish – the starters, mains, desserts, the cheese offer, the afternoon teas, the bread, the butter. He was a stickler for butter, always asking, 'Where's this butter from? It's awful. Get me some decent butter, never mind the cost.' Afterwards we would all go round the table to discuss everything we had tasted, analysing what would work, what needed improving, and then of course the costings as well, because it's vital to achieve the figures required. It was a full-on commitment.

There was also the Roux Scholarship. This is perhaps the most important competition for chefs worldwide, established by Uncle Michel and Dad in 1983. It offers the winner each year the chance to work a stage in any three-star Michelin restaurant of their choice. It is a huge honour – anyone who has won it carries an extraordinary stamp of approval that will be with them for their whole career. The competition encapsulates so much about the brothers' joint legacy: their care for the chefs of tomorrow, their insistence on technique and skill, their reverence for classical expertise. The competition is not just about good plates of food. It's about the person as well, and so the judges (my cousin and I took over from my uncle and father some time back) get ample opportunity to watch the chefs work. It starts with a written recipe and progresses through regional rounds before the final. To be a Roux scholar you need to be committed to teaching the next generation, and to buy into the philosophy that the brothers espoused: to be a great teacher, to be respectful of the industry, all of that. It may seem small because there is only one winner every year, but all the finalists will say that it has been a huge opportunity in their lives that they have benefitted from. And when you think of all the people that that one winner will go on to train – it's that trickle-down effect again, that dissemination of their work. It was a huge thing in both the brothers' lives and now feels like almost a crystallisation of their legacy.

~

There was never really a dwindling with my dad. Physically, towards the end there were some challenges. The years of hard work in the kitchen, combined probably with old injuries, meant that his legs gave him trouble. He had difficulty getting in and out of cars, or up stairs, but he didn't let that stop him. Mentally, he remained as strong as ever. Before lockdown hit in his last year, he had his routine. Get up, go to the office, work until lunchtime. That routine in many respects kept him going, kept him alive, because he had a purpose. So even if it took him half an hour to get up the stairs to the office, he would get up those stairs. We shared an office with Gordon Ramsay, and the number of times that Gordon would meet him on those stairs and say, 'Come on, Chef, let me give you a hand' – only to be robustly rebuffed by the old man. He wasn't going to let some stairs beat him. He'd get to the office, read his mail and get his work done and then invariably go for a business lunch. He still had all his old acquaintances and friends, and still needed to entertain prospective clients for big events. There was always something going on.

Some years after the divorce from my mother, and then the end of his second marriage, he found real happiness in the last years with Maria, his third wife. She was more than a match for him: someone he could bounce off, someone who could also hold her own in the kitchen. Outside his lovely flat in South London, he was still growing vegetables, and still keeping his kitchen in perfect order. He loved his life – he loved working, loved entertaining, loved his last beautiful dog, Canelou.

My main sadness is that the last year of his life, like that of so many others, was so affected by lockdown. It put a halt to his own daily routine, and of course was disastrous for our industry. We had to shut the doors of Le Gavroche for the first time in fifty-four years. For someone who had taken such pride in the fact that the Gavroche had been full every night since it opened, it must have been heartbreaking. He almost couldn't grasp it. He understood the gravity of it business wise, but couldn't get his head round why those decisions were being made. Every time I'd speak to him, he'd say, 'You're still shut? You're not allowed to open yet?', and I would try to explain to him the intricacies of furlough and suchlike and how we were trying to scratch a few pennies together by selling some wines. He would be worrying about the staff – what were they doing? How were they? To be forced into closure like that just didn't make sense to him.

And then there was the question of us being in lockdown and not allowed to give him a hug. The fact that he couldn't see anybody, and we had to tell him people couldn't come and see him. 'Why not?' he would demand.

'Because of the virus.'

'I don't care about this bloody virus!' I know he wasn't the only father in the country who reacted like that, but it was hard for him, and for us all.

It was wonderful when we were finally allowed to open, and he could at last come and dine in the restaurant again. He came several times, and saw the Perspex screens we had put up. He was delighted by that: 'How fantastic. They've really done a great job; you can hardly see them. Shame about the bloody masks though, because I can't hear anything!' Which was true – it is hard for some of our elderly guests who rely more on lip-reading. But I am glad he saw the restaurant thriving again.

The last time I cooked for him, I decided to do one of his childhood favourites. It was one of those moments when lockdown had at last lifted enough to allow the markets to be open and for us to visit, so I went to Brixton market and bought some honeycomb tripe – it's one of the places in South London where you can get proper fresh tripe (Tooting market is another). I cooked up a big batch at home, put it in some Tupperware and took it round. He was mostly in bed at that time, and his sight wasn't great. I took this container in to him and opened it up. He couldn't see it properly, but he could smell it. His eyes lit up. 'Where did you get that from?' he said, astounded.

'Dad, I cooked it for you,' I said. He was just over the moon with it. (Maria was slightly less so: 'You're going to stink the house out!') But he loved it. It took him right back to his roots. It was a very special moment. Whenever we eat tripe or *andouillette* now we always think of him.

But in truth I think of him often. And the images that come to my mind are the younger Dad, in full flight. Charging through the markets ahead of me when I was a young teenager. Or fishing, which was something we did together from when I was a very young age. Dad adored it. Not so much coarse fishing where you sit on a riverbank waiting for a bite – he didn't have the patience. But spinning, or catching live bait and fishing for pike: there was an adrenaline rush to that. Likewise, sea fishing. I remember going with him to a weir in Marlow on the River Thames when I was about twelve or thirteen. It was incredibly dangerous because the river there is a proper weir, lots of white water and a very fast current. The old man was in his element: keeping me safe while getting the most out of the fishing, 'Stand here, don't go there, you might fall in . . .' I can see him now, happy as anything on the riverbank. He loved being in nature – he was a countryman at heart.

I think of him playing poker after service when I was a young teenager doing some washing-up shifts at the old Gavroche. Very late on Saturday nights, after the last guests had gone and the cash tips had been distributed, Dad used to play a couple of rounds of poker with Silvano and the front-of-house team and sometimes the chefs as well. They would finish off the open bottles of wine, and the room would just be a haze of smoke, because everybody smoked and they would have brought out the cigars. And the old man would just sweep the table clean. The cash tips would all be his by the end of the night and he'd be triumphant. As a young teenager I wasn't allowed to join in and I certainly wasn't allowed to smoke, but I remember the laughing and swearing, and seeing wads of notes piling up ever higher in front of Dad while the others were crying their eyes out. Here they were, they'd just been all flush, and then suddenly the boss had won it all. That was the camaraderie of the place, all exhausted and elated from the night's service, ready to play some cards and share some laughter.

I see him manning the pass, in full sergeant major mode, bellowing orders and waiting for the call back, inspecting each plate of food with the most rigorous of eyes. A dictator in his kitchen, but a benign one.

It is a great shame that he didn't live to finish his book entirely, or to see it published. He would have enjoyed that. He would definitely have enjoyed celebrating the publication. I am sure there are so many more stories he didn't get time to put down on paper. But what he did write tells so much of who he was and what he did. It is moving for me to think of him as that young man, on the boat to England for the first time. Even more moving to think about him in Algeria – three years away from home, in danger. This was something he barely mentioned when we were growing up – he might tell the odd story, but he was very wary about glorifying that time. He had been proud to serve, but he didn't enjoy it. He didn't think the war was right. I think he wanted to shake it off. In happier times, it's interesting to see Gavroche coming together from his point of view, the challenges he faced, the speed of its success and the pleasure he took in it. You can see on the page some of the qualities that made Dad who he was – the energy, the humour, the drive. It was an amazing life.

Most of all, it is a joy to see running through the whole book all the lessons that I absorbed from him over the years. The value of enjoying what you do. The power of optimism and the willingness to work your socks off. And the importance of food – not just how to cook, or recipes for particular dishes, but the real worth of food. Food is not just fuel. Food is a joy. Food is life. Food can bring people together. If you look at that very first menu there are lots of sharing dishes, designed to be brought to the table and carved. That is very much the sort of ethos he espoused. He was always thinking of the togetherness and conviviality that food can bring. That is a way of being. That is something that my dad taught not only me, but the whole country. For that, I am both proud, and grateful.

35. The Roux family

From left to right:
Alain, Michel Sr, Albert, Michel Jr